AF485586

Math Heals

Math Heals

On the Gift and Weight of Being Human

Tiffany Suson

Math Heals: On the Gift and Weight of Being Human

© 2026 Tiffany Suson. All rights reserved.

No part of this book may be reproduced, distributed, or transmitted in any form or by any means, including photocopying, recording, or other electronic or mechanical methods, without prior written permission of the author, except in the case of brief quotations used in reviews or critical discussion.

For information, please contact: mathhealsmindset.com

Published by Avaida Publishing

Grapevine, Texas

ISBN: 979-8-9952930-1-9

LCCN: 2026906724

First Edition

Printed in the United States of America

This is a true story rooted in the author's real-life experiences and philosophical reflections. The events and examples presented are drawn from the author's personal reflections and observations. Names and identifying details may be altered to protect privacy. Any resemblance to other persons or situations is coincidental.

This work explores philosophical and structural reflections on life through mathematical language and analogy. It is not intended to diagnose, treat, cure, or prevent any medical or psychological condition.

BEFORE ALL THINGS

To God, the Author of all order,
the One who set laws in motion
and gave truth its shape.

*"For by Him all things were created,
in heaven and on earth, visible and invisible,
and in Him all things hold together."*

— Colossians 1: 16-17

To my husband,

for giving every equation of life its meaning.

To my children,

whose questions remind me that truth waits to be discovered.

To my parents,

for the life that made this one possible.

Contents

An Invitation

Appendices

Introduction

I never meant to finish my college algebra book that night in high school. I was only supposed to read and answer a few pages to prepare for class the next day.

After I read the lesson and answered the required questions, I opened the next page to see what the upcoming topics would be. I found myself reading those pages and solving the problems that followed, then the next, and then the next.

I was so absorbed in what I was doing that I did not notice the time passing.

When I finally reached the end of the book and looked up, it was morning. The sun was rising. I remember feeling afraid that my parents might catch me and discover I had not gone to sleep. I probably had only an hour to get ready for school.

Looking back, I sometimes wonder why I did not stop when I had already finished what was required. I should have felt relieved that the homework was done, but instead I kept going.

That is how math has always felt to me.

When I look at my children now, I sometimes wonder if it felt to me the way coding or online games feel to them today. It is that same kind of focus that pulls you in until time slips quietly past.

What I remember most clearly from that night was the strange state it left me in. It felt almost like a trance, the kind that comes from being completely immersed in something.

When I finally stopped, I remember feeling guilty instead, as if I had given myself too fully to something that was not supposed to hold that much of my attention.

In school, I was never especially strong in English or history. Math held my interest in a way the other subjects did not. Yet there has always been someone better than me at it, and that never bothered me. It was simply the subject that has always made the most sense to me.

It took me a while to notice that I was not only doing math in the classroom. I realized that my mind was also organizing the world in patterns.

When problems appeared in my life, I approached them the same way I approached a math problem. My attention often zoomed out first, trying to see the whole of a problem before moving closer again to the parts that could be understood. I found myself looking for what was known, what was missing, and what might allow the pieces to settle into place.

Somewhere along the way, I started asking myself a question.

If math describes so many systems around us, why does it seem to disappear when life becomes personal?

We trust math to build bridges and calculate distance. We rely on it to send rockets into space. Cause and effect shape many of the systems around us, even when we do not stop to notice them.

Yet when relationships strain or emotions rise, we rarely rely on that same logic. The moment begins to feel personal, and we act as though everything is falling apart and losing its order. Our reactions arrive quickly, and the search for understanding fades.

Problems rarely appear alone. They arrive with explanations, opinions, and the stories we tell about them. Emotions gather around them and make the situation harder to see clearly.

Often, I wondered whether moments like these could be approached the way we approach a math problem by looking for the order beneath what first appears confusing.

Because if math shapes so much of the world around us, why does it become harder to see when the confusion belongs to our own lives?

This book grew slowly from that curiosity.

Math gave me a place to pause.

When life became tangled, it allowed me to step back long enough to separate what I felt from what might actually be happening beneath the surface.

Sometimes that pause revealed how the situation was actually simpler than I first thought. At other times, it only showed me how little I understood. I am often humbled to realize that I am still learning.

There are days when the weight of things feels larger than I know how to carry.

In those moments, I find myself returning to the same question, the one that first appeared long before this book took shape.

What happens if I treat this moment like an equation and begin with what I know?

In math, beginning with what is known does not guarantee a solution. It only creates a place to start. The rest of the work comes from remaining with the problem long enough for its structure to reveal itself.

Life does not unfold on a chalkboard, and its variables rarely present themselves as clearly as numbers do.

Still, I wondered whether the same patience we use in math could help us see more clearly in the places where human experience feels most uncertain.

Are we really that different from everything around us that clearly follows math?

As the pages unfold, some ideas may return more than once. Math often reveals its patterns this way. A structure that appears in one place begins to appear again somewhere else, sometimes quietly and sometimes in ways that look completely different at first.

Similar patterns may appear outside these pages as well, in nature, in work, in relationships, and even in the struggles people face throughout their lives.

Perhaps we can simply look to see whether the same structure that math describes might also be present there.

What follows is not a set of answers.

It is simply an attempt to notice what might already exist.

That is where *Math Heals* begins.

Ratios shape the growth of leaves, and proportion guides the branching of trees. Balance holds ecosystems in place, while patterns appear throughout the natural world, from shells along a shore to the spiral of a seed. None of this asks to be noticed. The math holds whether we see it or not.

ORDER - WITNESS = TRUTH

Chapter 1

Order Without Witness

I used to think stillness meant nothing was happening. It often felt that way after a long day.

Two children arguing. A child crying in pain, sometimes screaming for no clear reason. Sudden screams followed by laughter cutting through whatever I was trying to finish. The television running while the dishwasher hummed and the washer and dryer ran at the same time. Toys hitting walls and furniture. My name being called again and again throughout the day.

I worked through my patient notes at the counter with all of it happening around me. My shoulders were tight, and my jaw was clenched without my noticing.

When I finished, the house seemed to grow quiet too.

The children stopped arguing. The appliances shut off. The rooms stopped echoing, and silence arrived.

For the first time that day, the house was still. It felt as though everything else had paused too.

Though the noise had faded, I noticed the tension still in my body.

I stepped outside, needing space to breathe. Just a moment when no one needed anything from me.

A flock of birds lifted from a nearby tree.

Their movement drew my eyes as they moved farther and farther away.

When I could no longer see them, the only thing left in my view was the clouds. I watched one cloud as it moved slowly across the sky, indifferent to my watching it.

I may have watched the clouds so long that they seemed to stop moving. It felt as though I was the one moving instead. Suddenly, I felt the ground shift beneath me and lost my balance, reaching for the deck rail before I had time to think.

That was when I remembered.

The Earth does turn.

Nothing had just started or stopped. I had simply become aware of motion that had always been there.

The planet rotates at more than a thousand miles per hour, yet we do not feel it because everything around us moves with it.

What I had thought was imbalance earlier in the day was not disorder. It was movement working together, just beyond what I could see.

The noise, the movement, and the constant interruptions were part of the same order.

They were parts moving at different speeds, sometimes colliding before settling into rhythm.

The body may appear still when standing upright, yet muscles adjust in small, unseen corrections. Ligaments hold tension. Joints shift by degrees too small to notice.

Balance is maintained through constant response. Nothing is frozen.

The Earth turns. The body compensates. The house hums.

What feels like upheaval is often movement trying to find alignment.

Stillness, I realized, is not empty. It is motion organized beyond what I can see.

The small routines that repeat each day, the habits I do not think about, and the breath rising and falling without instruction all form a structure I rarely notice.

I had assumed that nothing was happening when nothing appeared to change.

When the room was silent and my body was still, it felt as though everything else had gone still too.

Yet order continues whether or not it is noticed. Much of what holds the world together happens beyond our awareness.

A lake can look completely still. Beneath the surface,

currents move. Plants grow. Creatures follow paths that never appear above the water.

If the world existed without people, it would continue as it always has. The sun would rise and waves would move. Gravity would hold everything in place.

None of this waits for explanation.

Touch something hot and your body pulls back before your mind understands why. Plant seeds out of season and nothing grows.

Math is present in ordinary moments. In the rhythm of my steps as I walked back toward the house. In the way one small task led to the next. In how meals appeared when we were hungry and time stretched where it was needed.

Patterns appear everywhere. The spiral of a seashell follows the same ratio that shapes hurricanes and galaxies.

Our bodies move within structure too. Hearts beat in rhythm, and lungs rise and fall without instruction.

The world was already operating within structure long before human awareness entered.

Standing in my yard, I became aware of my own weight on the ground, the pull of gravity through my feet, and the way my breath rose and fell without effort.

My body was already participating in the same system as the sky, the birds, and the turning planet. Nothing about me was separate from it.

When I felt the world move beneath me, it did not create meaning. It revealed what had always been there.

An equation does not create balance. It describes it.

The equal sign does not force agreement. It simply shows that both sides align.

The same order that moves the sky also keeps my heart beating.

None of this depends on being observed.

———

If order stands without a witness, what changes when a human enters the system with choice?

An equation exists before we encounter it and remains unchanged even when we do. Nature moves within this order without hesitation, with growth and change following what is already present. Humans are the exception. We pause inside the equation.

BEING HUMAN = TRUTH + FREE WILL

Chapter 2

The Human Exception: Free Will

The planets remain in their orbits, and rivers still find their way to the sea. Nothing in nature pauses to consider what it is doing or why.

Humans, though, are different. We often hesitate.

In moments of uncertainty, I start to question the pattern. At times it feels as though something has gone wrong rather than simply unfolding as it should.

We trust equations to build bridges and send rockets into space. We rely on order every day. We calculate time and distance without thinking, and we plan and adjust constantly. These systems guide us quietly, even when we do not name them.

Yet when difficulty appears, we behave as though order no longer applies.

It is not that the rules stop working. It is that we hesitate to apply the same rules to ourselves.

When faced with difficulty, I find myself negotiating before anything has even begun. I imagine how hard it will be, how long it might take, and whether I am capable of seeing it through. Sometimes the decision to continue or step away is made before any action is required.

But it is not the equation that has changed. My willingness to continue has.

This kind of hesitation does not appear in nature. A tree does not calculate its distance to the light before it grows. It does not wonder whether it should take in water, and it does not avoid what nourishes it or debate what sustains it.

Without free will, experience would simply pass through us, the way wind moves through trees. But humans possess something nature does not. We can pause. We can consider. We can choose how to respond to what is in front of us.

This may be the human exception. We do not stand outside the equation, and we do not break it. We sit in the middle of it, choosing how to respond.

We can move away from what is true without ever leaving the system itself.

If free will exists within an ordered system, what happens when we begin assigning meaning to what we observe?

*The equation remains the same whether it is observed or not.
The numbers do not adjust to the person studying them. What
begins to change is the interpretation of the equation. The
structure holds, but the observer begins assigning meaning to
what is already there.*

TRUTH + OBSERVER = EXPERIENCE

Chapter 3

The Equation and the Observer

I remember one afternoon while homeschooling the kids. It was our science day, one of my favorites.

That day we tried something simple: two celery stalks placed in separate glasses of water, one dyed blue and the other red.

Before we set them down, I asked the kids what they thought would happen.

One thought the color would rise right away. The other said nothing would change.

Once the glasses were on the table, the waiting felt different. We were no longer just watching. We were watching for something.

At first, nothing seemed to happen.

I hadn't realized the experiment would take more than one day. The science lesson was supposed to be finished that afternoon. Our homeschool schedule was already set, and suddenly it had to be adjusted.

I felt a slight resistance rise in me, a small tightening that felt familiar. It was the discomfort of falling behind.

Part of me wanted to explain the outcome and move on.

But the celery was still doing what it needed to do.

They checked the stalks every few minutes. Both grew impatient, even though they had guessed opposite outcomes.

When the faint blue line finally appeared, one smiled, pleased to have been right. The other went silent.

The next day, as the color continued to rise and the veins became clearer, both of them leaned in close. Tracing the lines with their fingers, they pointed out where the blue deepened and where the red spread.

They were surprised that something they could not see before was now visible.

For a moment, neither of them cared who had guessed correctly. They were simply watching.

I handed them a small knife and let them cut one of the stalks.

Inside were tiny circles, each one filled with color. They held the pieces up to the light.

"So that's how it gets up there."

They turned the slices over in their hands, studying the patterns and offering their own explanations. One thought the water must be traveling through tiny holes.

The other said it looked like little straws pulling the color upward.

The color followed the veins already inside the stalk, rising slowly along paths that had always been there.

The change was slow and easy to miss. There was no moment when it suddenly began and no signal announcing its start.

Movement became visible only after enough time had passed.

It looked almost still, but it wasn't. Something precise was happening inside the stalk.

Watching it did not make it move faster, and stepping away would not have slowed it down. The process did not depend on our attention. It continued according to its own conditions.

Colored water was moving upward through the thin veins inside the celery, the same lines the children had just seen when they cut the stalk open.

What surprised me was how easy it was to forget what we had just observed once we left the table. Our attention returned to the rest of the day.

Even when truth stays where it is, experience does not. Two people can stand in the same moment and leave with different conclusions.

Sometimes the moment barely has time to arrive before I am already telling myself a story about it.

That is usually where things begin to drift.

I can argue with gravity all day, but the glass still falls. Action still produces results, even when I place meaning on top of it.

Simply seeing a pattern does not mean I can fix it. Sometimes it only shows me where I have been.

I see the same thing in my work as a physical therapist. People who have fallen before often become afraid of falling again. Sometimes the story begins before they even take the first step.

That fear changes how they move. Their steps become cautious, and their shoulders tighten. They brace as though the past is still present.

They are no longer responding only to what is in front of them. They are responding to what they carry.

Experience is not always the same as what is actually happening. Reactions and assumptions often arrive at the same time as the moment itself.

Observation alone does not resolve everything. Sometimes it only shows me how I have been responding to the situation. Some days I recognize this quickly. Other days I don't.

But the celery continues to draw water upward, and the body continues to adjust to keep its balance.

What is true does not change just because I notice it.

If observation can distort what is true, what happens when feeling arrives before understanding does?

When we first encounter a math problem, we begin assigning meaning to it: simple, confusing, difficult, or even impossible. The meaning assigned to the equation gives rise to emotion. Confusion, frustration, fear, or anger can appear before the problem has been worked through. Sometimes the feeling freezes us, and we begin to think there must be something wrong with the equation itself. Yet nothing in the equation has changed. Emotion, which was not there before, now stands beside the equation, describing our reaction.

EMOTION ≠ TRUTH

Chapter 4

The Problem of Emotion

There was a time when my three-year-old had a meltdown over pizza.

The first pizza had just come out of the oven, but he wanted the next one, the one with the toppings he liked. I kept trying to calm him down and explain that the pizza he wanted was already being made. I hoped he would understand if I just said it again.

"Give it ten minutes, and you can have the one you want."

None of what I said could reach him.

Lying on the kitchen floor in front of the oven, he was crying and shouting. He was trapped in how he felt, as if nothing else existed in that moment.

I stood there holding the plate, unsure of what else to do. Part of me wished he would stop for a second and look up, just long enough to see the answer sitting right there.

Another part of me wanted time to move faster so the next pizza would be done.

I wanted the noise to stop, the air to settle, the kitchen to feel still again.

Underneath all of it was guilt. He was hungry, and I could not give him what he wanted yet. I had offered him other things, but he refused them. Standing there, I felt a kind of helplessness, the strange weight of having a child in front of me who needed something I could not immediately give.

His emotions filled the room, and reason could not reach either of us.

Standing by the oven, I could feel how completely the space had been taken over by feeling. The tighter I held the plate, the harder it was to remember what I already knew.

The oven light stayed on. The timer kept running.

Nothing about the situation had changed.

In that moment, I wanted comfort more than truth. The truth that the pizza he wanted was not ready yet was the part that hurt.

I see how often I do this.

We soften reality so disappointment does not have to be faced. Sometimes we give in simply to quiet the noise. What is true remains where it is.

That moment showed me how easily feeling moves ahead of understanding. Emotion arrives quickly and claims importance before explanation has time to appear.

When feeling takes authority, it becomes harder to see the order beneath the moment. Feeling itself is not the problem. The difficulty begins when feeling replaces understanding.

I could feel myself wanting the moment to end before I fully understood it.

Feelings come fast. They announce that something is being experienced, yet they do not explain what that experience means. They point to impact, not cause.

Emotion does not show up on its own. It often appears when something in a situation has become complex. But reaction alone does not explain what is happening.

Discomfort is quickly labeled as something to fix rather than something to understand. The urgency to resolve emotion often replaces the work of seeing what came before it.

Moments like this showed me why math helped me think.

You cannot solve for x without writing the equation. You can guess, but you cannot verify. Two plus two remains four, whether we like the answer or not. What is true does not adjust itself to ease discomfort.

When emotion takes the lead, truth can begin to feel harsh even when nothing about it has changed.

If truth is set aside to protect feeling, the same problems return. The same arguments follow. The same pain appears again.

I see this when something breaks at home. Voices rise, explanations multiply, and blame follows. The simpler question of whether the problem can be fixed is often skipped.

Feeling fills the space while the causes behind it remain unseen.

Emotion does not resolve while reaction is active. It runs its course. Only after it settles can we examine what preceded it.

What is true does not soothe reaction, but it reveals what led to it.

I honestly do not think people feel too much. Often, feeling simply ends up leading.

Order still exists, but when feelings come first, life begins to feel unfair.

If feeling takes the lead, what happens to the mind's ability to stay with what is unfinished?

Not every equation resolves quickly. Some require time, repetition, and endurance before the answer becomes clear. Clarity does not always appear right away. Feeling rises in response to what remains unfinished. The equation does not disappear in the presence of uncertainty. It remains whether we stay with it or step away. Learning to remain with the equation becomes part of the work itself.

$$\text{CLARITY} = \text{TRUTH} \times \text{TIME} \times \text{ENDURANCE}$$

Chapter 5

The Unfinished Equation

My husband still dreams about being in math class.

When he wakes from the dream, his body is tense, as though the test never ended. He tells me it always begins the same way.

He is sitting in a classroom during a math exam. The board is already covered in equations they are supposed to solve.

Minutes pass. He works through one problem, then another, but several remain.

Slowly, one by one, his classmates begin to stand and walk their papers to the front of the room. The sound of chairs scraping against the floor fills the space.

He looks up at the clock and realizes how little time remains. His page is only half full.

Then the bell rings. He looks at the board, then back at his paper. The problem is still unfinished.

He always wakes before the solution appears. Even now, the dream stays with him. The panic is no longer sharp, but the feeling remains.

On the surface, it may seem like a dream about numbers, but what stayed with him was something different.

It was the experience of being inside a problem that had an answer but not enough time or clarity to reach it. The feeling of being left alone with something that did not yet make sense.

I wish I knew how to help him make the dream stop. I can sense how much it unsettles him when it happens.

Only recently did he tell me he had thought about asking me to teach him math, hoping it might quiet whatever still lingers from that classroom.

I had never offered because I did not realize that was what he needed.

I can still see it in his shoulders when he talks about it.

The feeling itself is familiar. Over time, I noticed how quickly emotion appears when something feels unfinished. The feeling itself is not the problem. It is information.

What happens next is where choice enters.

When a problem has no clear path forward and understanding has not yet arrived, it is free will that determines what happens next. We can remain present, or we can leave.

I see this surface during conflict. When tension builds between us, there are moments when he shuts down completely.

He grabs his keys and leaves without explanation.

Later he returns with ice cream, even though we are both committed to keto. He eats slowly, spoon by spoon, until the internal noise quiets.

The pressure lifts and, for a moment, the weight feels lighter. But nothing has been solved. The equation has not changed. It has simply been avoided.

In those moments, I can see clearly that he is responding to the same internal signal he felt in that classroom. It is the same discomfort of facing something unfinished while clarity is still out of reach.

It is free will that gives him the ability to step away, even though the equation itself remains.

But when he leaves, I am left holding what has not been said. I feel frustrated that he leaves before we can work through the problem together. The conversation ends without resolution, and I am left with uncertainty about where he has gone and whether he is safe.

What began as one uncertainty gives rise to another.

The unfinished equation stays with me while he is away.

What hurts most in those moments is how unfair it feels to be left alone with something we created together.

In stepping away, he has left me holding the very uncertainty he was trying to escape.

Many times, I want to fight back and force him to stay, to make him face it with me.

But I do not.

Instead, I end up sitting by myself, trying to understand how to make him see.

What makes it harder is that our arguments are usually about the same thing. It feels like solving the same shared equation again and again, where the resolution is clear but the other side is always left unfinished.

I stay with this unresolved equation while he steps away.

When he comes back, he has already consoled himself with ice cream. The edge is gone for him.

Even though he feels better, he does not want to talk about what went wrong. He does not want to return to the equation. He cannot understand why he should when he already feels okay.

And the unfinished equation remains with me.

There was a time when math trained us to stay with a problem.

Math involved more than arriving at answers. It required staying with the problem until understanding formed.

A solution could not be rushed. You had to sit first with the confusion long enough for the equation to reveal itself.

That struggle was part of the process.

A wrong answer carried information. The red mark beside it simply pointed to something that still needed to be seen.

Each attempt returned you to the same equation and built familiarity with imbalance and correction.

Confidence grows from continuing to work on the problem.

Math does not remove emotion. It allows emotion to rise while the equation remains the guide.

Over time, I began to see what that discipline quietly taught. It trained the mind to tolerate not knowing and to remain present with difficulty.

The lesson was simple. The answer exists. If it is not visible yet, something is missing.

Gradually, the ability to remain with what needs to be faced began to weaken. Being left with the unfinished became harder to tolerate.

And it started when emotion began to be treated as authority instead of information.

The incomplete equation started to feel unfair instead of unresolved.

That is where anxiety began to appear.

Discomfort came to mean there was no way forward.

Free will was used to leave instead of to stay with the problem, even though nothing about the equation itself had changed.

Nothing outside him forced him to leave. It was not the feeling that pushed him out the door.

It was free will.

He chose to grab his keys instead of staying with the conflict in front of us.

The interpretation that it was too hard, too uncomfortable, or unsolvable in that moment did not change what needed to be addressed.

It only delayed it.

The equation did not disappear because it was avoided. It remained where it was, waiting to be completed.

The dream ends before the solution because that is often where we stop in life as well. We leave while the work is still forming. We try to quiet the signal instead of finishing it.

The fear was never the equation. It was knowing that we would eventually have to face it.

Math teaches that truth does not vanish when we leave. The equation remains whether we are present or not.

Eventually, we stopped trusting that.

We began to leave when staying with what was unfinished became uncomfortable.

When an equation remains unresolved, what draws us toward comfort instead of endurance?

Correction helps us see where to look again in the equation. Discipline teaches us how to remain with a problem until it begins to make sense. But along the way, comfort begins to matter more than the goal of understanding. Eventually, reassurance replaces correction, but it does not solve a math problem. The work must still be done. If it is avoided, the answer remains out of reach.

COMFORT − CLARITY = INSTABILITY

Chapter 6

When Comfort Replaced Clarity

I remember when math felt like a way of strengthening my mind.

Learning took patience. I stayed with what I did not yet understand until it began to make sense. Struggle did not feel like failure. It was how I learned where to look.

What mattered was whether the pieces finally fit.

The structure of classrooms began to change. Phrases like "There's no wrong answer" or "just do your best" started appearing where discipline once lived.

I grew up in a time when showing your work did not earn partial credit. If the answer was wrong, it was wrong. Precision mattered.

Looking back, kindness may have been what changed the direction.

I started to notice that students were no longer learning to look for what was true in the same way. They were learning to look for approval.

I have seen how easily the mind begins chasing reassurance instead of clarity. When that happens, it forgets how to stand on its own.

Some teachers no longer use red pens because red is said to be too harsh. Purple or green replaces it.

That red mark once meant something simple.

It said, "This part is not right yet."

It was never meant to shame. It showed us where to look again.

We softened the mark to protect feelings, and in doing so we lost something important. That red mark gave direction. When it disappeared, so did a kind of clarity.

This appears in small moments. When we disagree, it is now common to apologize first. We grow careful with honesty, afraid it might sound unkind.

I find myself doing the same thing, wrapping truth in reassurance so no one feels hurt.

We try to make things easier for the people we care about, believing we are helping.

I have learned, often the hard way, that difficulty is sometimes the very thing that allows growth to happen.

Early in my career, one of my hardest lessons was learning to let patients work through difficulty. I remember watching other therapists guide patients through challenging movements and feeling uncomfortable. At times, it felt unkind.

I wondered if it was simply a difference in culture. Perhaps because I am Filipino, stepping in to help quickly felt natural to me.

As I worked with patients, I began to see what changed when effort was allowed to happen. I began to understand.

They were not being mean. They were protecting the process.

In my work with patients, I help them rebuild strength and learn to move on their own when it is safe.

I eventually began to see that recovery depends on effort. Muscles do not strengthen through comfort. Balance does not return through rest alone.

I tell my patients to walk every hour when it is safe for them to do so.

Sometimes I learn that a family member has been bringing them whatever they need, trying to be supportive. The intention is pure, but the outcome is not.

The patient stays seated all day, never discovering that comfort is what keeps them weak.

I understand why caregivers do this. Stepping in feels faster and kinder.

But each time we intervene too quickly, we interrupt the very process that would have made them stronger.

I have learned that empathy does not always mean removing effort. Sometimes it means staying close while allowing the effort to unfold.

It was like the night my husband left after an argument to get ice cream.

He was not hungry, and it was not about dessert. He was trying to calm what had not yet settled.

It made him feel better. He seemed calmer when he returned.

But the imbalance remained.

The feeling eased, yet the problem was still there.

I still wonder whether we fix things, or whether we simply become better at quieting the noise.

I return to that question often. Some days it is hard to tell whether peace has truly arrived, or whether we have simply learned how to carry what remains unresolved.

Somewhere along the way, discomfort became something to avoid. We moved from correcting to consoling, believing this was compassion.

I have watched how protecting people from correction quietly removes the very process that helps them grow.

Peace arrives when the moment finally makes sense and the tension settles.

I witness this often at home. I watch confidence build when I allow difficulty to do its work.

I see it in my children when I step back while they struggle with something challenging, stacking blocks that keep falling or learning new chords on a guitar.

I remember another afternoon when my daughter was working through one of her online lessons.

The program moved step by step. After each lesson, a short quiz appeared. If the quiz was not passed, the lesson simply started again. The system would not allow the student to move forward until the quiz was passed.

Before long, I heard frustration in her voice.

She told me she had already gone through the same lesson several times, but the program kept sending her back. Each time she reached the quiz, it returned her to the beginning.

I walked over and sat beside her.

When the next question appeared on the screen, I told her quietly to slow down and read it carefully. As she moved the mouse across the answers, I could see she was still rushing. Her eyes skimmed the screen, and her hand moved quickly.

The cursor stopped over an answer that clearly did not match the question.

For a moment I watched her finger rest on the mouse. I could see the impatience in the way she hovered there. I did not stop her. I let her click.

The program responded the way it always does.

She did not pass.

The lesson restarted, sending her back through the same reading and video lesson again.

She sighed and leaned back in the chair. I knew there were clothes in the laundry that needed folding, but I stayed there next to her and waited.

Eventually she reached the quiz again.

When the question appeared, I reminded her once more to slow down.

This time she paused. She let out a long breath and read the question again, moving her eyes across the words more than once.

A few seconds passed.

Then her face changed.

"Oh," she said quietly. "I get it now."

She clicked the answer.

This time, the program allowed her to move forward to the next lesson.

She smiled slightly and returned to her work.

Peace arrived the moment the answer aligned.

If comfort can ease a moment without correcting it, what brings the same problem back until it finally changes?

When a math problem is difficult, we sometimes step away from it for a while. We return later with clearer eyes. But the equation has not changed. It remains as it was when we left it. Truth does not change while we are away. It simply waits where it is, without pressure. There is grace in math.

LOVE = ORDER × GRACE

Chapter 7

The Order and Grace of Math

The kitchen was quiet.

Two of my children were sitting at the table doing their homeschool lessons while the baby slept in the other room. For a while, the house felt still. It was one of those rare days when everything around us seemed calm. Even then, I could tell my son was carrying noise inside him that he could not quiet.

In front of him sat the same algebra problem he had been staring at for some time. The page was covered in pencil marks and faint eraser smudges, the kind that come from trying more than once.

I waited, unsure whether I should step in. I could feel my own impatience rising, wanting the moment to resolve so we could move on with the rest of the day.

The equation was still there, unchanged. Waiting for him to see it demanded patience from me as well.

He looked up and sighed. He said he had done everything the way he was supposed to, but it still did not make sense. The answer kept coming out wrong.

I watched as his focus faded. His shoulders sagged slightly, saying more than his words ever could.

I walked over and leaned in. Tracing the steps with my finger, I saw where he had moved too quickly.

$$x + 4 = 12$$

$$x = 12 - 4$$

He had written:

$$x = 9 \; ✗$$

There it was. One small misstep.

Writing nine instead of eight.

A single line rushed past, and the answer unraveled. Because of that small misstep, nothing that followed could be correct. He had followed the structure but moved too quickly to notice the detail that mattered.

He paused and stared at the page.

Then I saw it happen.

The moment understanding returned.

His shoulders relaxed, and the air in the room seemed to settle. By then, the answer mattered less. Approval was no longer what he was looking for.

What arrived instead was the peace that comes when something finally aligns.

Grace had been waiting there.

It took a while, but the answer had been there the whole time.

In that moment, I understood how math teaches grace.

After that afternoon at the table, I began thinking about how often this appears outside of math.

There was a season in my life when waiting felt much heavier.

A year after we got married, my husband moved to the United States while our eldest son and I remained in the Philippines. The plan was simple: once the priority date arrived and our papers were approved, we would follow.

At first, it was easy to hold. Our son was doing well, enjoying time with his grandparents and extended family. I was working. Life felt full enough where we were.

Over time, people began asking why we were still there, when we would be leaving, and whether something had gone wrong.

At first, I brushed it off.

But as the years passed, the questions kept coming, and slowly they worked their way inside me. The strain showed up between us. Some days, I questioned where it was all going.

Eventually, I decided to move things forward myself.

I gathered my papers and began applying to employers in the United States. I sent applications wherever I could until I finally found someone willing to hire me and sponsor a work visa.

Four years after we were separated, we were reunited.

Then, almost all at once, the original priority date arrived, allowing the petition we had filed years earlier to move forward. Around the same time, my husband became eligible for naturalization, which would have made the process even faster.

Only then did I see it.

Even if I had done nothing, the process would have begun moving forward around the same time.

The outcome we had been waiting for had not changed.

I had simply changed the path.

I do not regret the way it unfolded, but I learned something important.

Sometimes we act because waiting becomes uncomfortable. We change variables because the silence feels too long. But what is already in motion does not disappear when we grow impatient.

It remains where it is.

It works the same way in life.

We notice a mistake in someone else, whether it is a friend, a child, or a coworker, and our first instinct is to fix it.

Sometimes grace means holding back and letting the moment breathe.

Truth does not move while we wait. It simply gives space for someone to see it for themselves.

Two students can work through the same problem using different approaches. One writes equations. The other draws a diagram. Both arrive at the same answer.

The paths are different, but the truth stays the same.

Outside the classroom, we move the same way. One person forgives quickly. Another needs time before speaking. One works things out by talking. Another works things out by stepping back to think.

We move at different speeds.

Understanding still waits.

Grace allows for those differences without forcing one pattern.

There is a student who keeps missing the same kind of problem on every quiz and still does not give up.

Each time the teacher circles it and writes, "Try this one again."

That same question waits for him on every page.

Until one day it finally clicks.

Grace shows up there too.

Not in getting it right the first time, but in the chance to return.

We promise to listen better, to be more patient, to slow down, and still forget.

Growth rarely happens in a single attempt. It forms through small corrections repeated over time.

That return happens without shame.

The bell rings while a few students are still writing. The teacher gives them a moment longer.

The rules remain firm, but there is room for understanding to catch up.

That counts too.

When we fall behind or miss what we thought we had, something sometimes reappears. A conversation we thought was finished. An apology that comes later than planned. An opportunity that returns when we are finally ready.

Grace does not erase structure.

It gives us time to meet it.

Two plus two still equals four, no matter who writes it down.

That reliability offers safety. The rules do not change depending on who is answering.

Outside the classroom, that consistency matters too. We miss things. We take wrong turns. And still, what is true remains true.

Sometimes grace is nothing more than time. We do not have to change what is true to make things fair.

You can see this kind of grace in nature. The tides rise and fall without hurry. The Earth stays the right distance from the sun. A tree bends with the wind and returns when the air settles.

Balance appears when things are allowed to realign, not when they are forced. Some days, I notice it quickly. Other days it takes longer. Either way, it waits.

If truth is constant while we come and go, how do we recognize misalignment the moment it appears?

In an equation, a result either holds or it does not. Sometimes we sense that before we can explain why. When the equation holds, the structure is aligned. When something is off, the equation no longer balances. That signal draws attention to what needs closer examination. When followed carefully, it leads back to the variable that needs adjustment. Eventually we begin to see that emotion is not part of the equation.

$$\text{PEACE} = \text{TRUTH} \times \text{ALIGNMENT} \checkmark$$
(emotion as confirmation)

$$\text{PEACE} \neq \text{TRUTH} \times \text{MISALIGNMENT} \times$$
(emotion as signal of imbalance)

Chapter 8

The Purpose of Emotion

I remember sitting in that math class, certain I had worked it out correctly. I had checked each step twice and felt sure of myself. But when the paper came back, there was a single red mark, an ✗ beside the number I had written.

It was just a mark, but it landed heavier than I expected. My stomach dropped and my chest tightened as disbelief moved through me, followed by doubt. My body reacted before my mind could catch up.

The mark was only asking me to look again. It was not accusing me. Still, all I could feel in that moment was failure. I stared at the page longer than I needed to, as if the answer might change if I waited.

That moment happened years ago, but the feeling has not changed.

It is the same drop in your stomach when bad news lands. A call from the doctor. A text that changes everything. A door you thought was open but remains closed. The body feels it first, long before the mind understands. It is that mark you feel before you know what changed.

The checkmark ✔ arrives just as suddenly.

A small symbol that means you got it right. Your shoulders drop and you let out a breath without noticing. For a moment everything falls into place. The answer aligns, and with it comes relief.

Life gives us those same moments. The message comes and the words calm us. The results are clear. They made it through surgery. You got the job. The air feels lighter.

We might call it joy or relief, but underneath those names is the same truth.

Emotion confirms alignment. It is the body's first response when truth is contradicted or confirmed.

That is when something else became clear. Emotion rises fastest when the equation becomes complex. More variables. Unknown outcomes. Higher stakes. Delayed results.

The system is still calculating. But instead of showing a pause or delay, we feel it.

Emotion is what that rapid estimation feels like inside a human body when clarity is missing.

It is similar to how the body alerts us when something moves out of range.

When blood sugar drops, we feel shaky or weak. When temperature changes, we sweat or shiver. When oxygen is low, breathing changes.

These are not the problem themselves. They are signals telling us there is something we need to look at more closely.

I realized emotion follows the same pattern.

It appears when something in the internal equation no longer balances. It signals that the equation is incomplete.

Maybe we do not avoid math in life because life is too complicated.

Maybe we avoid it because we keep solving the wrong thing.

We try to solve emotion.

We treat feeling as the variable, when it is not part of the equation at all.

Emotion is feedback. It reveals whether the equation is balanced or incomplete.

Once I saw that, everything rearranged.

I realized emotion was not the problem that needed fixing. It was the signal showing me where to look.

I gradually began to notice how much emotion guided my attention. Without it, I would not have known when something inside the equation was off. It was often the first sign that something in the structure needed attention.

Emotion no longer feels like noise to me. It feels like the system letting me know something is out of balance.

When I saw a mark beside my answer in math, I did not stay there hoping it would change. I went back and looked at the steps to find where something moved too quickly or a detail was missed. Even with a checkmark, I would glance again, curious about what worked.

The mark was never the lesson. The process was.

In life, I noticed I sometimes did the opposite.

Even though emotion pointed toward something that needed attention, I sometimes lingered inside the feeling instead of returning to what came before it. I replayed the moment, hoping the discomfort would fade on its own.

I called it sadness, anger, or disappointment, but underneath it was the same signal asking for attention.

Emotion points toward what still needs to be seen. When we stop there, the imbalance deepens. What could have led to clarity turns heavy. The correction still waits quietly while we keep staring at the mark.

In math, when you do not see where the mistake happened, you are likely to repeat it. The problem shows up again, giving you another chance to notice what you missed.

That is grace.

As soon as something hurts, our instinct is to make the pain stop.

I have done this many times. Scrolling on my phone. Starting a random project. Cleaning just to stay busy.

Those things help for a moment. But the equation remains.

I think of that night when my husband went out for ice cream after an argument. The sweetness helped briefly.

What needed attention was still waiting.

In physical therapy, pain eases not by silencing it but by restoring balance. A muscle may hurt because it is compensating for something out of alignment.

Stretching what is tight and strengthening what is weak takes patience. Discomfort often means something is finally changing.

Avoidance does not resolve what is stuck. Movement does.

Emotion works the same way.

There was a time when mornings felt heavier than they should have. Dropping kids off in different places. Calls from daycare in the middle of work. Schedules colliding.

It was almost as if the pattern we had adapted to began to carry more weight. What once made sense gradually did not feel right. Many days I found myself wondering why I felt the way I did, trying to find the variable that might be off. I did not yet realize that the conditions themselves had changed.

An equation that once held no longer balanced.

I remember driving to a patient when the call came. My stomach tightened. My son was sick again.

I started doing the math in my head. Could I finish the visit, pick him up, take him to the doctor, and still make it back before his sister's daycare closed?

By the time I hung up, I felt the weight of it.

At the same time, my husband was doing his own calculations. Leaving work meant moving patients' appointments. If he stayed, I would have to go. We would lose income while still paying for daycare.

No matter which variable I adjusted, something was lost. My emotions rose as the structure of my life no longer fit this particular time.

I tried to keep going anyway. Some mornings, I woke already tired. It showed up as impatience and exhaustion. Underneath both was a slight resentment I did not want to name.

I noticed that when I ignored what emotion was pointing toward, it did not fade. It returned until I was willing to look.

Emotion was not asking me to judge myself or anyone else. It was drawing my attention to a structure that needed to change.

Sometimes emotion confirms alignment. Other times it signals misalignment.

Either way, it is not meant to lead. It points.

The feeling does not define who you are. It brings your focus back to what is real, to what truth has been waiting for you to see.

If emotion is only the mark beside the work, what does correction look like when two people share the equation?

In math, apologizing for getting a problem wrong does not change the answer. Until the wrong variable is corrected, the outcome remains the same. Words may ease the moment, but the equation does not respond to apology. It resolves only when something in the structure changes.

FORGIVENESS = ALIGNMENT VERIFIED OVER TIME

Chapter 9

The Math of Forgiveness and Time

My mother once told me she had tried going days without speaking to my dad, hoping silence would communicate what words could not.

But my father did not operate that way. He said what he needed to say, reached his clarity, and moved on. Within hours he was speaking again as though the moment had resolved. He did not return to the argument.

Once the equation made sense to him, the feeling had nothing left to attach to. The problem had already been solved.

For a long time I thought that meant he did not care. Later I began to understand it differently. He was not avoiding the problem. He had already corrected it in his own mind.

While others stayed in the tension, he had already seen enough to move toward resolution.

I am similar in that way. My calm does not come from hearing "I'm sorry." It comes when something is set right.

When truth is restored, emotion fades on its own. Forgiveness, I realize, often arrives when understanding catches up.

But not every system closes that quickly.

Even after the season when my husband left and our son and I stayed behind had passed, something in me kept solving a problem that no longer existed. I carried the fear that it could happen again.

In moments of conflict, I would return to that season, bringing it back into conversations where it no longer belonged. The structure had changed, but my body was still calculating probability.

Sometimes when he promises something now, my mind returns to that earlier season and quietly recalculates the likelihood. I remember the promise he made then and how it did not happen. I remember being the one who had to carry it instead.

Even when I know logically that it was not his fault, something in me still hesitates. I hear his words but measure them against that memory.

It was not separation I feared.

What stayed with me was the weight of a promise that had not been kept.

Each time I found myself returning to the equation, quietly testing whether the variables would hold this time.

The equation itself had already been resolved.

What lingered was the memory of instability.

What I did not understand then was that my body was waiting for proof. It was watching for consistency, gathering repeated results to confirm that the conditions had changed.

As life continued without separation returning, the probability slowly decreased. The fear gradually loosened as alignment held over time.

Forgiveness came through verification. This is how many natural systems recover.

After a storm, even when the rain stops, the ground remains soft. Stability takes time to return because systems need repeated confirmation that the conditions have changed. Roots take time to trust the ground again. Water drains and soil settles. Nothing else needs to be added.

Correction happens first. Strength follows later. That same pattern was unfolding in me.

People naturally look for patterns. When the same variables produce the same result again and again, the mind begins to recognize stability. We call it reliability. We call it safety. Often we simply call it trust.

What we are recognizing is consistency. The pattern holds, and the system no longer needs to keep solving the same uncertainty.

I also learned that not every equation resolves.

Years ago, someone told a lie and chose not to correct it. There was no acknowledgment and no attempt to restore what had been distorted.

For a long time I carried anger, believing the imbalance belonged to me simply because I was the one feeling it.

That person and the lie they told stayed in my thoughts for a while. I kept turning it over, trying to balance an equation that was never mine.

I replayed conversations, searched for explanations, and looked for ways to fix something I did not break.

Eventually I realized that the equation was never mine to correct. Time did not repair it. Time clarified where it belonged.

Forgiveness there did not come from waiting. It came from recognizing that I could not correct an equation someone else refused to complete. My responsibility was to keep my own side aligned with truth and allow the imbalance to remain where it belonged.

I eventually began to see that forgiveness has more than one form.

Sometimes forgiveness appears after correction has already happened but the body needs time to recognize that safety has returned. Sometimes forgiveness comes when correction never happens and time reveals that the imbalance was never yours to carry. And sometimes forgiveness arrives quickly when understanding closes the loop right away.

Time shows which is which if we are willing to notice.

We often say "forgive and forget," but forgetting is not something we command. Memory settles when the system stops predicting harm. That outcome only happens through consistency over time.

Forgiveness is not an emotional act. It is the result of alignment being proven.

This is why "I'm sorry" often feels unfinished. Words may soften a moment, but unless something actually changes, the equation remains the same. Apologies can ease tension, but they do not restore balance.

Real peace appears when truth replaces what was wrong and time confirms that the correction holds.

When correction never comes, peace appears in a different way. It arrives when we keep our own equation aligned and release what we were never meant to solve.

Time does not heal by itself. Time reveals. It shows whether an equation has truly been corrected. It shows whether safety has returned and clarifies when imbalance belongs elsewhere.

Forgiveness becomes possible once that truth is known.

If time reveals whether alignment holds, how do we learn to recognize when an equation is truly complete?

When giving moves in only one direction, the equation begins to lose proportion. Even when intentions are good, one side of the equation starts carrying more weight than it should. Over time, the imbalance becomes visible as the ratio begins to change. Strain gathers where one side continues to give while the other receives. Balance returns when each side of the equation carries what belongs to it.

$$\text{LOVE} = \text{TRUTH} \times \text{PROPORTION}$$

Chapter 10

Ratio of Love

One of my children has always been the responsible one. She notices things before anyone says anything. If a sibling needs help, she is already there. If I look busy, she comes over and asks if I need something.

Helping has always felt natural to her. At first she did not think much of it. If something needed to be done, she simply did it. Over time she became the one people looked for. No one ever said that out loud, but it became understood.

One day she asked why she was always the one being asked to help, and why her older brother was not. She was not pushing back. She was simply trying to understand what she was seeing.

There is often someone who gives without stopping: a friend who is always available, a coworker who never says no, a parent who never really rests.

Their hearts are sincere and their intentions are good. They believe that love means giving, and that giving more means loving more.

At first it feels aligned to give. It feels right. But when giving has no proportion, it slowly begins to take more than it returns.

The person who keeps showing up begins to disappear inside the equation, slowly losing their own place while continuing to carry everyone else. Every act of giving changes the math.

When what goes out is not balanced by responsibility and truth, something subtle begins to form. It does not begin as anger or resentment. It begins as a quiet sense that something is off.

It appears in a quiet sigh after saying yes one more time when we are already tired. It surfaces in thoughts we do not say out loud, in moments when we begin to wonder whether anyone notices the effort or whether it has simply become expected.

Even while reminding ourselves that we are being kind, somewhere inside we can feel that something is uneven. For a long time that feeling may go unrecognized as imbalance.

Some people give freely without keeping score. They do not count favors or remind others what they have done.

The problem is not the act of giving but what happens when the supply runs out. The imbalance becomes visible when nothing remains and the expectation to give continues.

Resentment rarely appears while we are giving. It begins when there is nothing left, yet giving is still expected.

Somewhere along the way, giving out of love begins to feel assumed. When nothing is left to give, the absence of giving can begin to be interpreted as not loving.

Often we do not see the change while it is unfolding. Others may notice first and point out that too much is being carried. Even then it can be difficult to understand how it could be too much if we are still capable of giving.

Eventually it becomes clear that the pain does not come from being asked or even from giving too much. Sometimes it comes from no one seeing when the giver has been depleted.

The system had no signal for capacity. The requests continued even when nothing was left to offer. Any system without a limit will eventually collapse under its own demand.

Emotion did not create that imbalance. It revealed it. Just as pain alerts the body to injury, resentment alerts the equation that balance has already been lost.

Nature corrects imbalance in the same way. A tree does not try to save every branch. When a limb grows too heavy or stretches too far, it eventually breaks.

From the outside this looks like loss, but the tree does not collapse when a branch falls. It survives by redistributing weight and preserving resources. Growth continues where it can be sustained.

That is correction.

Even small moments show how this works.

One morning my children asked what they were supposed to bring for their homeschool co-op lunch. I told them I would be making sandwiches for all four of them. Two of them immediately protested. They did not want sandwiches.

I explained calmly that I could not cook four separate meals. The issue was proportion. If one person is responsible for four different outcomes, the system loses balance.

They sat quietly. Then the older two stood up, walked into the kitchen, and decided to make their own lunches.

That choice corrected more than the meal. Responsibility returned to where it belonged, and there was no need for argument. Everything settled back into place.

Whether the problem was a lunch, a marriage, or a misunderstanding, peace arrived when each person held their own variable.

Love begins to collapse when responsibility becomes one-sided. Giving that once felt natural slowly becomes depletion.

Love holds its shape only when both sides are supported. When balance is present, giving feels natural instead of draining. It begins to feel more like rhythm than sacrifice.

Peace often feels like this.

Love and logic are not separate languages. They move together. Without proportion, love begins to drift. Without compassion, correction loses warmth.

Love requires structure as much as it requires kindness. Every equation still requires balance.

Forests make room for new growth when old trees fall. Rivers change course when banks erode. Bodies rest when muscles fatigue.

Only humans try to override depletion. We keep giving past zero. Most of us were never taught when to stop.

Some people learn to give without losing themselves. They forgive while holding limits. They stay honest even when it is uncomfortable. They do not twist truth to keep others comfortable. They do not dilute what is real to avoid conflict.

They remain aligned.

This is the ratio of love.

If growth requires balance, when does responsibility return to the person who still holds the choice?

Life does not suddenly become harder because something went wrong. The equation has not disappeared. The variables have changed. What once felt manageable begins to carry more weight as variables accumulate. The structure remains, even as the equation grows more complex. Sometimes that change is simply growth.

EQUATION × CHOICE = GROWTH

Chapter 11

The Equation of Growth

Sometimes, just when life feels like it's falling into place, something new shows up. Suddenly, the equation that felt stable a moment ago is out of balance again.

At some point, life can start to feel like we're making the same mistakes over and over. The situations change. The people change. But the tension feels familiar. The variables change, but the pattern repeats.

Frustration creeps in, and we tell ourselves we should know better by now. We expect growth to make things easier. Instead, the problems feel heavier. The consequences stretch further. What once resolved quickly now lingers.

There are days when it feels like growth has failed. But what if it hasn't? What if the variables have simply changed?

I think back to when I first learned math. At the beginning, there was addition, then subtraction. Later came multiplication and division.

Each new skill felt harder than the last, but the problems themselves stayed simple. You always knew where to start. If you made a mistake, it stayed small. You erased it, corrected what went wrong, and moved forward.

As I grew older, the math didn't disappear. It layered itself. Addition and subtraction no longer stood alone. Multiplication appeared inside larger expressions.

Eventually, the problem stopped telling you which operation to use. You had to recognize what was being asked, then decide how to begin.

Missing a step mattered more and rushing carried consequences.

Each choice shaped what came next.

Growth in nature follows the same pattern.

When a plant is young, shallow roots are enough. A small amount of water sustains it. Wind may bend it, but it usually holds.

As it grows taller, the conditions change. The soil must support more weight. The wind applies greater force. What once held it upright is no longer sufficient. The equation still exists, but the load has increased.

Nothing about the environment has become hostile. The structure remains. It is only that the demand increases.

That is when I noticed something.

Balance does not maintain itself. Someone still has to hold it.

This is when I first began to notice free will in real time. It stopped being an idea and became something I could feel.

I saw how quickly emotion stepped forward and took over. We dress it up with words like honesty and passion and call it authenticity. Emotion stepped forward and tried to solve the equation by itself.

Emotion is loud. It convinces us that reacting is the same as being authentic and that intensity equals freedom.

Often, emotion was the one leading.

What surprised me was how peace sometimes returned when I paused. Emotion did not disappear. It simply stopped driving.

I could feel something without obeying it. In that space between what I felt and what I did next, clarity returned.

That was when free will returned.

Healing did not come from changing my feelings. It came from deciding what they meant.

When we are young, decisions are immediate. Emotion leads because experience has not yet taught proportion.

As we grow, life adds variables. We meet new people. We carry outcomes longer. We begin to see patterns. Probability enters.

Our actions start to ripple outward. Somewhere along the way, the question shifts from "Can I?" to "Should I?"

Those years, especially adolescence, are filled with that tension. Freedom gets tested. Limits get discovered.

Over time, I noticed that free will changes how it shows up. It stops trying to escape structure and begins choosing it.

Truth no longer feels like restriction. It starts to feel like direction.

Wisdom did not arrive suddenly. It settled in quietly after I stopped trying to force the outcome of the equation.

Peace began to grow where control loosened its grip and proportion returned.

Emotions still appeared, but over time they found their proper weight.

I am at the age now where I can see growth happening around me, not as theory, but as a pattern.

I have a toddler, a grade schooler, a middle schooler, a high schooler, a young adult, my husband and me in our forties, and a mother in her seventies.

Each of us is living inside a different version of the same equation, solving for different variables.

My toddler lives in cause and effect. Want, wait, receive.

My grade-schooler is learning about fairness and patience.

My middle schooler is learning proportion, how to measure feelings against the moment.

My high schooler is balancing independence with consequence.

My young adult is learning alignment. His choices now carry real outcomes.

He is discovering that freedom is not the absence of boundaries. It is the proper use of them.

My husband and I are still working inside equations we thought we solved years ago.

Ours now include work, children, time, and the future. There are more variables, more patterns to notice, more probabilities to consider.

The math is unchanged. We still pause. We still measure. We still correct instead of explaining away our reactions.

And then there is my mother. Watching her reminds me that growth does not end with youth.

Years alone do not bring alignment. Reflection does. Some equations repeat until truth is finally seen.

As I grow older, I notice that my problems do not disappear. They become more complicated.

Sometimes I look at my children and wish I carried only the problems they hold now.

Other times, I wish they would never feel the weight of the ones we carry as adults.

There are days I hide my struggles from them, not because I'm pretending everything is fine, but because I want them to stay free of worries that aren't theirs yet.

Seeing them all at once made something clear.

Every stage of life has its own math.

The toddler solves for patience.

The teen solves for consequence.

The adult solves for alignment.

Different numbers. Same structure.

Free will began to appear quietly through all of it. Each of us decides whether to react or remain aligned.

Some days we give in to how we feel. Other days we pause and move differently.

Growth lives there, not in having the answer, but in what we do next. Choice is what moves the equation forward.

I came to understand that reclaiming free will does not mean becoming less emotional.

Emotion became a signal to me, like a checkmark ✔ or an ✗ on an exam.

It shows me where to look. It tells me something is right or something is off.

But it is not the equation.

When emotion quiets, even slightly, free will returns.

It takes what we feel and decides what it means.

From there, I can step back and see the equation instead of being trapped inside reaction.

I did not grow by shutting down emotion. I grew by listening to what it pointed toward.

Anger marked crossed boundaries. Sadness gathered where something had been lost. Joy appeared when alignment returned.

Each feeling found its place when free will held it.

Over time, urgency eased and a pause appeared. Listening began to replace reacting, and decisions slowed.

I learned how to stand inside emotion without being governed by it.

Growth became visible not because difficulty disappeared, but because of how I began to move through it.

If growth begins when we choose to work through the equation, what happens when we mistake one variable for the outcome itself?

In mathematics, an outcome is rarely produced by a single number. The same result can appear through many different combinations. When one variable is treated as if it alone carries the answer, the outcome becomes fragile. When that single point changes, the entire result can seem threatened. Yet the equation itself has not disappeared. The structure still holds, even when the variables move.

$$\text{OUTCOME} = X + Y + Z$$

Chapter 12

When We Attach to One Variable

We were already in bed when my husband finally said what had likely been sitting on his mind all day.

"If we're trying to secure our son's future," he said, "then I probably need to make more money."

He sounded certain, as if he had already solved it in his mind. For him, money meant security.

There was nothing wrong with that. It is how most of us are taught to think. If you want security, you look for the variable that seems to produce it and try to manage it.

Still, I paused. My eyes drifted to the ceiling as a question began forming.

Then I turned toward him.

"Is money actually the outcome we want," I asked, "or is the outcome a secure future for our son?"

He didn't answer. He stayed quiet.

I lay there thinking. My mind kept turning the question over, the way I do when I simplify an equation to see what is really inside it.

"If what we want is for his future to be secure," I said after a moment, "money could be part of it. But it doesn't feel like the whole picture."

He turned toward me.

I hesitated, trying to find the words to explain it better, then tried again.

"Think with me for a moment," I said. "What if we're jumping to the variable instead of naming the outcome?"

I started to recognize attachment as the moment when we mistake one variable for the outcome itself.

He waited.

"I mean," I said, searching for it, "think about it like an equation. Say x plus y equals five."

He didn't interrupt.

In this equation, five is the constant. It represents the outcome we want. What we don't know yet are the variables.

In a math problem, the constant is the number the variables must reach.

$$x + y = 5$$

"If the total is five," I continued, "there isn't just one way to get there. It could be one plus four. Or two plus three. It could even be one plus two plus two. Five stays the same. The variables change."

Knowing the equation exists doesn't solve it. It just means the effort isn't random.

We could both see that money might still be one of those variables. It just didn't have to carry everything.

Once the constant was named, the variables stopped feeling like burdens. They began to feel like possibilities.

The outcome remained constant while the parts could move, combine, or change in ways we couldn't yet see.

Yet the mind often believes the entire equation collapses when one part of the equation fails.

We believe that if money doesn't come in, his future isn't secure. If development is delayed, his future isn't secure. If support never forms around him, his future isn't secure.

Emotion rises not because the future has changed, but because the mind has tied it to a single path.

I noticed how easily we demand certainty too early, not because the equation requires it, but because we do.

When the mind loosens its grip on a single variable, something unexpected happens. It doesn't fall apart. It settles. Space opens.

Possibilities begin to appear that were always there but hidden behind our insistence.

"If our son grows in maturity and learns to care for himself," I said, "that's a secure future."

I wasn't thinking about careers or savings accounts. I was thinking about whether he would feel safe in his own life.

He nodded.

"If a support system forms around him through people, programs, or resources," I continued, "that's a secure future."

He nodded again.

"What if his future ends up being secure in a way we don't see yet?"

He exhaled slowly. I could feel him beginning to release the idea that he had to design the solution himself.

I find that when I fixated on one path, everything narrowed. I began telling life how it had to unfold instead of paying attention to what was already forming.

Money didn't disappear.

It simply returned to its place as one variable among many.

When my peace depended on one variable, it became conditional. I monitored and tried to control, not because the outcome was truly at risk, but because I had placed responsibility for it entirely on myself.

That night, something eased, even if nothing was solved.

My husband's concern for our son didn't vanish. What changed was where the responsibility rested. When it stopped resting on a single path, the tension began to release. There was no longer a need to force it.

Nothing around us had changed, but the way we were looking at the variables had. I realized peace didn't come from trying to get the future right.

But deep down, I could feel our understanding of the variables beginning to change in both of us.

It appeared when truth was allowed to sit where it belonged.

If the outcome stays the same, what happens when no single variable can carry the equation anymore?

Sometimes an equation does not fail because it is wrong, but because a variable is still missing. We may repeat the steps and try harder, yet find that the equation still does not resolve. The answer does not come from doing more of the same steps. It comes when the missing variable finally becomes known.

KNOWN VARIABLES – MISSING VARIABLE =
INSTABILITY

Chapter 13

When the Equation Breaks

Our son was in distress. He would cry uncontrollably, scream or shout, and sometimes hit, without any pattern we could recognize. Even within what we understood about the autism spectrum, something in his body wasn't right. His stomach was often bloated. He passed gas constantly. There were days when he cried for no clear reason at all. Most nights, his sleep was so broken that he would wake and run into our bedroom again and again, until we were all exhausted.

At the time, we didn't know what we were dealing with. We only knew we couldn't keep living this way.

Looking back, this was when we began paying attention differently, even though we didn't realize it yet. We stopped seeing everything as behavior and started wondering if something else might be happening inside his body.

It took time to find a doctor willing to look deeper. When we finally did, we paid out of pocket and drove long distances, telling ourselves it was worth it even if nothing came of it. When the doctor walked us through the lab results, identified deficiencies, and shared a plan, I remember feeling relieved to have numbers instead of guesses.

But we couldn't follow the protocol.

Our son couldn't take the supplements and the medicine our doctor had prescribed for him.

We tried everything. Mixing them into food. Hiding them in drinks. Using tools his therapist suggested. Each time, it worked briefly, just long enough to give us hope.

Then, around the fifth day, everything intensified.

What started as refusal turned into screaming, crying, and throwing whatever he could reach. He would try to run outside the house simply to get away from it, without any sense of danger in his body, only the need to escape. We were always afraid we might lose him in a moment like that.

One morning, he spat everything across the kitchen floor.

It felt like watching everything fall apart in real time.

Every variable was being applied, and nothing was holding.

Everything his body had already been struggling with became louder once we started.

But stopping didn't fix what had sent us there in the first place. His bloated stomach, the gas, the crying that seemed to come from nowhere were still there, waiting.

At first, I thought we needed to try harder.

Instead, the harder we pushed, the worse everything felt. His body stayed braced, as if he were constantly preparing to fight or flee. Our home grew less peaceful. The urgency we carried began showing up everywhere. Meals were rushed. Our voices shortened. What was meant to help became something we prepared ourselves for.

It felt like driving with a warning light blinking on the dashboard, knowing something was wrong but not knowing how to fix it. It was like seeing a red ✗ next to a wrong answer on a math exam and realizing we were still trying to solve the problem the wrong way.

We had to face what we'd been avoiding. The way we were doing things wasn't working, and we had run out of ideas. Every attempt to force it made life harder for all of us.

Walking away from that approach felt painful. It felt like letting go of the only option we had left.

But once we stopped, I could finally see more clearly.

The protocol itself wasn't wrong. It just didn't fit where our son was.

The equation didn't have what it needed to hold.

We were trying to help his body settle without realizing that there was still a missing variable.

What we wanted hadn't changed. Our son still needed support. But we were starting out of order.

My husband believed we needed help from someone who understood what was happening. I believed that until our son felt safe in his body, nothing else would matter.

By then, he didn't trust what we were trying to give him anymore. We were aiming for the same outcome, but we weren't starting from the same place.

At first, it didn't feel like a real problem. Over time, it separated us.

Each time our son refused the prescribed supplements, one of us pushed forward and the other pulled back. Our conversations shortened. We stopped checking in the way we used to. Everything felt urgent, and we were afraid of getting it wrong.

From the outside, we probably looked like two parents doing everything we could. Inside, it felt like we were working from different equations. We weren't solving things together anymore. We were watching each other, quietly wondering who was right.

I realized I had become more focused on defending my approach than understanding what was actually happening. He was doing the same. We were tired and afraid we were going nowhere.

If we didn't pause and return to the same equation, this would stop being about the treatment.

I saw it in how we spoke. In how quickly we withdrew. What was pulling us apart lived underneath the situation itself.

I couldn't see it while I was caught in my own frustration.

Our son's overwhelm wasn't only his. It was already moving through the whole system of our family. When his body was overwhelmed, his emotions followed. From there, the rest of our family life lost its balance. Our communication changed. And the less connected we were, the harder it became for him to settle.

Over time, the whole house began adjusting around him.

Our plans and conversations depended on how his body was handling the day. So did the attention our other kids received. We stopped knowing what to expect.

That was when something clicked for me.

We weren't dealing with isolated problems. A family isn't just individuals living side by side. It behaves like a system, where each person becomes a variable in the same equation. When one part struggled, the rest of us adjusted around it. None of it felt random anymore. The pattern was starting to become visible.

The equation was still there. It just wasn't balanced. The bloating, the refusals, the meltdowns, the broken sleep all pointed back to the same place.

Seeing it this way, I stopped blaming him. I stopped blaming my husband. I stopped blaming myself.

The system was simply responding to something we hadn't accounted for.

And once I could see that, I knew the answer wasn't going to come from forcing harder. It was going to come from finding the variable that actually belonged in the equation.

At the time, it didn't solve the problem, but it changed where we were looking.

A system cannot stabilize when a necessary variable is missing.

If something essential is missing, how do we begin when we don't yet know what it is?

When a variable is missing, the equation does not stop existing. It remains incomplete. In those moments, the task is no longer to produce an answer but to determine what is missing. Problems begin to resemble equations being worked, where each attempt reveals information about the structure. Some values hold. Others fail to satisfy the conditions of the equation. Certainty is not always available. Free will moves away from trying to control the outcome and toward testing variables, observing the results, and allowing the structure of the equation to reveal what belongs.

UNKNOWN VARIABLE + TEST = INFORMATION

Chapter 14

Testing The Unknown

By then, I could see that we were no longer working with a single equation.

Our son was bloated and in pain, and still nutrient-deficient. The plan was the protocol our doctor had prescribed to help his body.

But inside that equation was another variable: he couldn't take the supplements.

What looked simple on paper unraveled in real life.

Everywhere I turned, someone was sure they had the answer. Some people warned me away from Applied Behavior Analysis (ABA) completely. Others said it was the only thing that helped. I read articles late into the night and listened to parents whose children had improved. I also listened to adults who spoke about their own experiences growing up with therapy they wished had never happened.

I didn't want to force anything on my son again. At the same time, I was afraid of holding him back from something that might help him. The more opinions I carried, the heavier it felt, as if choosing the wrong variable could change the direction of his future.

There were months when choosing a variable felt harder than leaving the equation untouched.

I kept returning to the same research, reading the same stories, hoping something would finally make sense. Most days, it felt like I was back to guessing all over again.

I began asking for help wherever I could.

I went to his speech therapist, hoping she could work on swallowing or oral sensitivity. She suggested a book.

We asked our occupational therapist, thinking she might understand the sensory side of it. She gave us strategies, and we tried them, but nothing held.

Each attempt carried hope. Each one ended in the same place.

Somewhere in the middle of all this, I noticed something in myself. I had suspected from early on that regulation might be the missing piece.

If his body could settle, taking the supplements for his deficiencies and medicine for his stomach issues might become possible.

When I asked around, more than one parent told me this wasn't the role of an ABA therapist. Giving supplements and medicine wasn't something they handled.

I hesitated.

And then I kept asking anyway.

We applied to one ABA program we thought might be a good fit. After a brief meeting with our son, they told us they couldn't take him. They tried to soften it by saying he was a superhero.

I remember standing there, holding that word in my hands.

It was meant kindly. It didn't help. It felt like another door closing.

By then, we were exhausted. Every option seemed to arrive with both hope and disappointment. My husband and I were still aiming for the same outcome, but we were carrying it differently. Each refusal made the path feel narrower.

Still, I stayed with the question.

If I refused something without testing it, was I acting from the equation or from fear?

So I kept asking. I kept explaining. I kept searching for someone who was equipped to help him regulate so he could eventually take what he needed.

Eventually, we found another ABA provider.

When I explained our situation, they didn't hesitate.

They said yes immediately. They told us they knew exactly what they were doing. They were willing to incorporate supplement tolerance into his treatment plan.

There was no buildup. No convincing.

Just a simple yes.

While that didn't solve everything, it changed what was possible.

A new variable would enter the system, and we would watch what happened.

When a variable brought more distress, I stopped calling it a mistake.

I started calling it information.

When something showed promise, we stayed with it.

I used to think that when something didn't work, my time and effort were wasted. It felt like walking the wrong road and ending up nowhere. But even what didn't fit still clarified what we were working with.

It reminded me of solving a Sudoku puzzle when only a few numbers are filled in. You place a number and watch what it does to the rest of the grid.

Sometimes you want to keep a number simply because you are tired of starting over.

But the grid doesn't bend.

When a number throws the system off, you remove it and try again. Slowly, the correct structure reveals itself.

In nature, something similar happens. Trees scatter thousands of seeds, but they do not expect every one to grow. Most never become trees.

Yet none are wasted.

Some enrich the soil. Some support other life. A few find the exact conditions where they belong and begin to grow.

When I insisted on keeping a variable that didn't belong, instability showed up. I used to call it stress or confusion, but it was feedback revealing that the variable didn't fit.

Free will, I realized, wasn't there so I could control outcomes. It was there so I could keep choosing and learning.

Every new option became another variable to test.

When something brought stability, it stayed.

When it created confusion, it didn't always last.

Most of what I learned came from trying something and observing what happened. I carried doubt with me and still do. But I stayed open.

If testing reveals what doesn't fit, what begins to happen when a variable finally does?

After testing, there comes a moment when the correct variable enters and the equation holds. Alignment does not come from force. It appears when the structure of the equation supports the outcome the system requires. Resistance becomes information. Instability begins to settle. Healing becomes possible when each variable returns to its proper place in the equation.

ALIGNMENT + STRUCTURE = HEALING

Chapter 15

When Alignment Appears

When we stopped forcing solutions, the problem did not suddenly resolve.

We had been turned down by the first ABA program, so starting again meant new applications, new paperwork, and waiting for space to open. When our application with the second provider was finally accepted and they were able to give him a spot, nothing moved quickly. There were weeks when all we could do was hold what we knew and wait. It was difficult to feel calm or confident. I didn't know what the next step would be.

Up until then, every refusal had felt like failure. Every setback felt personal, as if we were missing something important or doing something wrong.

Eventually, I realized that what looked like resistance was information. Our family wasn't unraveling. It was responding to something that didn't fit yet in the equation.

Once we began working with this ABA team, we found a different kind of support, one that didn't try to push past his reactions or override them. They treated his resistance as information rather than defiance. They moved slowly and watched carefully. Their focus wasn't control. It was regulation.

The changes didn't arrive all at once. They showed up quietly in everyday moments.

The therapists introduced the steps during sessions, and we continued them at home. We started small. A soft gel capsule that he could hold, then bring closer, then touch to his lips, with no pressure to swallow. His doctor-prescribed B12 spray was diluted into juice and increased gradually over time. Every step followed the protocol we had been given, adjusted based on how his body responded. Nothing was rushed.

And then he reached the point where he could swallow a larger capsule without resistance.

That was when I understood something I hadn't been able to see before. Healing showed up once the structure could carry it.

It wasn't because the protocol had changed, and it wasn't because his willpower had suddenly grown stronger. It happened because the equation could finally hold. Trust entered the system, and his body stopped fighting what was meant to help it.

Balance doesn't come from pushing harder on the wrong variable. A solution only holds when every part of the equation is in the right place. If a piece doesn't belong yet, effort alone won't make it work.

Once the right variable entered, the rest began to settle. The work no longer felt as heavy.

The changes appeared in ordinary ways. Our son's body was calmer. His focus improved. His mornings no longer began in distress.

And without either of us naming it, my husband and I felt something we hadn't felt in a long time.

We had space again.

The urgency we had been carrying, that constant pressure that everything depended on fixing this immediately, began to loosen. There was nothing left to push against.

My husband noticed the changes too. He watched our son take his prescribed supplements calmly, stay regulated, and wait between steps. He didn't analyze it emotionally. He could simply see that something in the system had settled into place.

We didn't arrive at peace because we finally talked everything through or agreed on every detail. Peace arrived because we were no longer pulling in opposite directions. We were responding to the same variables.

It was only then that I realized we had been forcing a variable into the equation. I assumed that we should know how to do this by now because we already had older children. I believed our experience would carry us through whatever came next.

But the equation didn't respond to the variables we already knew.

Once the therapists entered the system, the structure changed. They understood patterns we were still learning to see. They adjusted variables slowly, watched for feedback, and moved only when the equation allowed it.

Our son responded to that clarity.

And as he began to trust the process with them, he began to trust us again too.

In math, a problem can feel impossible until the right step appears. Once that step becomes clear, the rest of the work often moves more smoothly. The solution that once felt distant begins to come into view.

Once the right step appears, the rest of the equation can begin to resolve. Other variables that had been waiting for stability finally have a place to enter.

At the same time, the cost of everything had been quietly piling up. The testing. The therapies. The supplements. We were doing everything we could to help our child, and financially it was becoming harder to carry, especially during the months when it still felt like nothing was working.

Then, once things began to stabilize at home, something else became visible.

Support started to appear.

A biomedical treatment scholarship came through. Not long after, we received help that covered speech and occupational therapy. Later, our ABA program encouraged us to apply for a local grant, and when we did, it helped with copays and deductibles we had been carrying quietly for a long time.

None of it came from pushing harder or asking louder. We weren't campaigning or scrambling. It felt less like something arriving suddenly and more like something finally having a place to land.

The timing made sense to me. Healing hadn't begun because help arrived. Rather, once things began to stabilize, we could recognize the help that had room to enter.

It didn't feel like gaining more. It felt like becoming able to receive without collapsing.

For a long time we had tried to force the answer. The equation had been asking for something else.

We didn't create peace by forcing outcomes. We returned to peace by responding to what was already true. Once the structure of the equation held, everything connected to it began to reorganize. It didn't happen all at once, and it wasn't flawless, but the pattern slowly became recognizable.

If alignment can hold one equation, what changes when attention enters the next one?

*Sometimes the equation does not change. The observer does.
The variables remain. The structure remains. What changes is
which parts of the equation we finally recognize. Awareness
does not create truth. It reveals it.*

ATTENTION + TRUTH = AWARENESS

Chapter 16

The Observer Turns Inward

I remember being very young, probably around eight, watching the people around me and carrying a question I could not explain.

Why could they see me while I could not see myself the way they did?

At first I wondered what it would be like to step into another person's awareness, or if that was even possible.

Only later did I realize that I could see the world only from where I stood. I could not stand inside another person's view. I could not see through my own eyes what they saw from the outside.

Other people could see what I could not. They could see me.

I would look at mirrors and think about the difference between reflection and perspective. A mirror showed me my surface, but it did not give me access to what anyone else actually saw.

Even then, I noticed something.

There were things each of us could see that the others could not.

The equation itself may remain the same, but what an observer can see depends on where they stand.

An observer inside a system cannot see the entire system at once. Some variables are visible from one position but hidden from another. The structure does not change, but the information available to the observer does.

Attention determines which variables the observer can see.

Over time I began to recognize that life often works in the same way.

Sometimes the variables are visible and the situation seems clear, yet the conclusion still does not change.

Every situation has variables, both around us and within us. Emotion can signal that something has changed, but it does not organize the equation. Understanding begins when we look closely at the structure of what is happening.

One evening my husband noticed that my cellphone was uncharged.

At home it is usually my daughter who uses it. She talks to her friends, and sometimes uses it for online homeschool work. Because of that we had already been reminding her to make sure it stayed charged.

So when he saw the dead phone, he assumed she must have been using it excessively.

She had forgotten to charge the phone before, so he assumed the same thing again. If the phone was dead, she must have used it.

This time however, one of the variables was different.

Our daughter had not been home during the period in question. She had been at homeschool co-op the entire day, where phones are not allowed. The timeline made it mathematically impossible for her to have been using it.

The data did not support the assumption.

When I pointed this out calmly, the response was not uncertainty. It was certainty of another kind.

"She's done it before," my husband said. "So it makes sense she must have done it again."

In that moment the structure was visible. The timeline was clear. The inconsistency was obvious.

The math was undeniable, yet the truth it revealed was ignored.

Either we update the equation with the new information, or we keep the earlier conclusion even though it no longer fits.

The equation itself did not force either outcome. It simply showed that a decision was being made.

The disagreement was not what stuck with me.

What stuck with me was the realization that attention itself changes what an observer can see.

When attention turns inward, the observer becomes part of

the equation. When it does not, the equation continues forward with missing variables.

If attention changes what we notice, what patterns begin to appear when we finally turn it inward?

Some equations make sense in isolation. Others only become clear through repetition. Understanding begins to form as observations accumulate and patterns emerge. Repeated results begin to carry information. Clarity appears once enough results have been observed.

PATTERN + ACTION = ALIGNMENT

Chapter 17

When Patterns Become Visible

Our lives are filled with variables, conditions, and outcomes. When we pay attention, the structure of the equation becomes visible.

For several years, our lives followed a familiar rhythm. We lived in the state where we had raised our family. Our eldest had spent most of his life there, and his siblings were born and spent their early years there as well.

My husband and I did the same kind of work, and our oldest child, who was in college at the time, worked at the same company.

Our routines were familiar. Work shaped our days. Home shaped our evenings. It wasn't something we analyzed at the time. It worked, and because it worked, we trusted it.

Only later did I realize how much I had assumed that rhythm would continue unchanged.

In that season of life, the equation seemed simple.

Work + Effort = Stability

As long as that equation held, it stayed invisible. We showed up to work, did what was required, and were paid. We took care of our children. Life moved forward.

There was nothing to solve because nothing seemed wrong.

That began to change when the state introduced a new requirement tied to continuing our jobs. The requirement went directly against our values. At first, the weight of that did not fully register.

What we did not understand immediately was that the requirement was not limited to one employer. It applied across the entire state. Remaining where we were would eventually mean accepting it.

Leaving one job would not solve the problem. The equation was larger than a single workplace.

Work + Effort + Violated Values ≠ Stability

Policies change. Workplaces adjust. I assumed there would be some way to remain where we were without crossing a line we were not willing to cross.

Then the questions began.

Could we continue working under these conditions? Would our jobs still be available to us? What would happen to the life we had built if this requirement stayed in place?

I remember how unfair it felt. We had worked without complaint for years. We showed up when conditions were difficult. We adjusted when the work was demanding and, at times, unsafe.

We did what was asked of us. And now, despite everything we had given to the work, we were being told we could lose our jobs.

The fear was real.

How would we care for our children? How quickly could stability disappear?

Those feelings came before we understood the full situation, but they were not random. Looking back, I can see that emotion was responding to something that no longer aligned, even before my thinking understood it.

Emotion = Feedback

At the time, we focused on what seemed practical. We looked for exemptions. We contacted people who had the authority to approve exceptions. We asked questions, followed instructions, and submitted what was required.

Each step felt reasonable. Each one carried the hope that this might be the option that worked.

When the responses came back, they weren't what we hoped for. Each answer landed hard. At the time, all I could feel was the disappointment.

Exemption Request + Policy Requirement = Denial

Only later did I realize that the responses were consistent and that consistency was telling us something.

At first, I treated each response as its own event. Maybe this request would be viewed differently. Maybe the next person would see something the others had missed.

We stayed hopeful, not because the situation supported it, but because it felt too early to stop trying.

Over time, though, the repetition became harder to ignore. No matter who we talked to or how we asked, the answer stayed the same.

Only later did I recognize what was happening.

Repetition = Pattern

That was the moment the situation stopped feeling personal. It was no longer about who we were or how long we had worked there. The response did not change with explanation or effort.

The pattern itself had become information.

By then, the discomfort had already done its work. Looking back, I can see that it had been drawing attention to something that no longer aligned.

Despite all that, what followed was not panic or urgency. It was clarity.

I decided to resign from my job first. It was not easy, but the equation no longer balanced. Staying meant accepting a compromise we could not sustain.

Our oldest resigned soon after. By that point, the pattern had already made itself clear.

My husband stayed briefly. When his exemption was eventually reviewed, it was denied as well. I remember realizing in that moment that the response did not add new information.

It simply matched what had already been shown.

After his exemptions were denied, his employer asked whether he wanted to reconsider and remain by meeting the requirement. His answer came without hesitation.

The equation was already clear.

We packed our things and sold the only house our kids had ever lived in. Leaving the state was the only way to remain aligned with what we believed.

What I remember most now is not the disruption, but what came after. The calm did not arrive all at once, but it settled gradually. Once the decision was made, the unease faded. The questions stopped circling.

The emotion that had been signaling misalignment no longer needed to press for attention. We were no longer forcing ourselves to remain inside something that no longer fit.

Only in hindsight did I understand what had been happening all along. We stayed aligned with our values, and what no longer aligned began to rearrange our life on its own.

If the same outcome keeps repeating, what begins to carry more weight than effort or intention?

Once structure becomes visible, direction begins to appear. Over time, consistent variables begin to produce predictable outcomes. The future develops from what is already in motion. By the time outcomes can be observed, they have often been forming for some time. What feels like uncertainty is often simply the time between cause and effect. When we cannot measure what is happening, confusion increases. And when the equation behind the moment is recognized, clarity appears.

Truth × Time = Probability

Chapter 18

Probability, Hope, and the Future

The teacher asked a question out loud, casually, and the room responded as though it should already know the answers.

How many license plates are possible if each plate has three letters and three numbers?

At first, hands went up quickly.

Answers were called out with confidence. Someone guessed a few hundred. Someone else said a few thousand. Each answer sounded reasonable, close enough to feel right.

The teacher shook her head and said no.

More hands went up, and the numbers grew larger. Tens of thousands. Hundreds of thousands. The room stayed alert, but the mood began to change as the guesses sharpened and people began explaining their answers before being asked, as if justification might help.

Still no.

Confusion spread across the room as people looked around. Some stopped raising their hands altogether. Others raised them again, this time hesitantly. A few laughed a little too loudly. Someone said it must be a trick question. Another said there probably wasn't a real answer. Someone else asked whether letters could repeat, whether numbers could repeat, or whether the problem was even possible to calculate.

Eventually, most people stopped trying to answer at all.

The question had not changed. The reaction had.

The anxiety in the room did not come from the question itself. It came from not knowing how the problem could be measured. You could feel it in the way the room went quiet without settling, like everyone was waiting for something to land and nothing did.

I was sitting there watching this happen.

I knew the answer, but more importantly, I knew there was an equation behind the question. While everyone else stayed inside the guessing, I sat quietly, observing.

I remember thinking that if I hadn't known the structure, I would have been inside it too, guessing and adjusting, wondering why nothing seemed to work. Knowing there was structure changed what I could see, but it didn't make the room any less uncomfortable.

What stood out to me was how long it went on.

Wrong answer after wrong answer, with no interruption. The teacher didn't step in after the first few mistakes. She let the confusion stretch.

I felt uneasy. It felt strange to be calm in a room that wasn't calm. It felt like standing still while everything around you kept accelerating. I kept wondering why she didn't stop, why she didn't explain, why she allowed the guessing to continue when it was clear the room was spiraling.

I wanted someone to get it so we could move on, so the tension would finally release.

Eventually, I leaned over and quietly told my friend the answer. She raised her hand, and when she said it out loud, the room went still.

The teacher smiled.

Only then did she begin to explain.

It wasn't the answer that changed everything.

It was the moment everyone realized the question had structure. Relief moved through the room as people leaned forward, confusion softening as what had felt chaotic a moment earlier began to organize itself.

Nothing about the problem itself had changed. Only its structure had become visible.

That moment stayed in my memory because it revealed something I would notice again later. The anxiety in the room didn't come only from uncertainty. It came from the absence of measurement. When everything felt equally possible, the mind reacted as if it were under threat.

This is how the future has often felt to me.

When structure isn't visible, imagination opens every door at once. Possibility multiplies, fear drifts toward the most unlikely outcomes, and emotion reacts as though every imagined future carries the same weight.

What overwhelms us isn't uncertainty itself. It's the absence of measurement.

Probability appears when truth is carried forward through time. Not all at once, but gradually, as the same conditions keep holding and nothing interrupts them. It isn't guesswork or optimism. It's what becomes visible when direction begins to narrow.

A weather forecast doesn't list every storm that could form anywhere in the world. It reflects what is most likely based on existing conditions, tracking what is already developing rather than everything that could exist.

When life holds a consistent pattern, direction begins to appear in the same way. What once felt random starts to show shape, and over time, that shape begins to carry weight. Truth repeated through time doesn't create chaos. It shows direction.

Peace often begins to appear when we stop focusing on everything that could happen and begin noticing what is already set in motion. But sometimes something interrupts what is already unfolding.

Loss can interrupt it.

Something once present disappears, and emotion reacts as if the entire equation has collapsed. For a long time, that was all I could see.

Only later did I begin to notice that loss often marks the moment when truth becomes visible.

There are times when we feel at peace simply because nothing has challenged our assumptions yet. Comfort can hide structure. When loss arrives, what had been concealed moves into view.

Years ago, I believed our family was complete. We had one child, and we felt settled in that belief. Then, in a single moment, at a routine OB-GYN visit, I was told I was pregnant and that I was losing the baby.

At first, the loss felt like subtraction, something taken, something closed. Emotion responded immediately. It took time before something else surfaced beneath that reaction.

I realized I did want another child. It wasn't that the desire had disappeared. It had been there all along, unmeasured and unnoticed.

The loss didn't remove something from me. It revealed something that was already present.

I began to notice this pattern elsewhere. A seed beneath the soil is already becoming. Roots form before anything appears above ground, and systems engage long before results are visible. Delay doesn't signal failure so much as order unfolding at a pace we can't yet see. Truth doesn't disappear during waiting. Time multiplies it.

The same thing happens in daily life. Someone begins eating in a way that supports health, and nothing changes at first. The scale doesn't move. The mirror offers no confirmation. Internally, inflammation decreases and hormones begin to rebalance, while the probability of change increases long before the outcome appears.

Stability works the same way. When the structure is sound, time carries the equation forward. What seems small at first begins to matter as the pattern continues.

Peace in this middle space doesn't come from seeing the end. It comes from recognizing that the equation is sound and allowing time to complete its work.

Just as a tree doesn't lift its roots each morning to check its progress, alignment doesn't need to be disturbed simply because results haven't appeared yet.

When truth is in place and time is allowed to operate, probability produces outcomes emotion could never force.

There were moments when peace arrived before anything else had changed. I didn't trust it at first. Only later did I recognize it as a signal that the equation was already working.

There is a kind of peace that comes only after everything resolves. The diagnosis changes. Debt clears. Relationships stabilize. That peace depends on results.

There is another kind of peace that arrives earlier.

I've noticed it often comes right after emotion rises and then settles, when the possible futures begin sorting themselves instead of competing for attention.

Sometimes it feels like recognizing the ending of a story halfway through. Not because it's predictable, but because the structure has already revealed itself.

When my husband chose to take a job in another state before his exemption was denied, that same calm arrived. When the denial finally came, I felt relief rather than surprise. The outcome had already taken shape.

Emotion looks for certainty before resting, scanning for signs and proof. Peace grounded in probability rests sooner, recognizing that when truth moves through time, outcomes follow structure even if they haven't arrived yet.

The question becomes less about "What if this doesn't work?" and more about recognizing that the process has already begun.

Peace isn't the end of the journey. If anything, it arrives earlier than expected, becoming the first indication that the future is already moving, even if its shape isn't visible yet.

If probability is truth in motion, what happens when you realize that you are not watching the equation unfold, but living inside it?

Some changes do not stay where they begin. When one part of a system changes, the rest of the system adjusts. Effects may appear far from the original change. An equation does not always resolve where it begins. Sometimes it moves outward through the system, adjusting the structure around it as it settles.

TRUTH × STRUCTURE × CONDITIONS = SYSTEM ALIGNMENT

Chapter 19

Living Equations

I used to think life happened in separate moments.

One problem here, one decision there, one season ending before another began. That was how life was spoken about, and I assumed I was seeing it the same way.

Everything felt as though it arrived in pieces, disconnected from one another.

What puzzled me about life was the way it was divided. Even then, I kept noticing how one thing led into another, how a change rarely remained contained to where it began. I didn't yet have language for that. I only knew that the way events were separated never fully matched what I was noticing.

Watching our son struggle brought that difference into focus.

What we were living through did not stay contained inside his body. His dysregulation moved outward, into our home, into our sleep, into our conversations, and into how we made decisions. When his nervous system was overwhelmed, the rest of us adjusted around it, often without realizing we were doing so.

Our schedules bent. Our expectations adjusted. Our other children adapted in ways they had never had to before.

That was when it became harder to keep thinking of life as a series of isolated events.

I realized that I had always looked at life this way, even before I understood it. My attention moves outward before it narrows. Instead of starting with a single detail, I begin wide and watch how the details affect one another.

When something changes, I wonder where the effect will appear next. A change inside one cell becomes a sensation. That sensation alters the nervous system. The nervous system shapes behavior. Behavior reshapes a relationship. A relationship influences a household, and the household rearranges the rhythm of work, learning, and place.

I don't experience these layers as separate. They feel continuous, like the same equation appearing at different scales.

Watching our son, it became clear that what looked like a single struggle was already moving through many levels.

No equation stands by itself. Each one exists inside another. A nervous system is an equation within a body. A body becomes an equation within a family. A family enters the equation of work, community, and place. Each layer carries its own conditions, but none of them operate alone. When something is altered at one level, it enters every equation it touches.

A family is a system in the simplest sense: a set of connected parts where a change in one part changes how the others behave.

Our household reorganized itself around whichever element was most unstable, not because something was wrong, but because pressure always moves toward what can hold it.

We had been looking at our son as if he were the problem. What I began to see instead was that the balance of our home now centered on his regulation. Everything else arranged itself around that condition.

Once I could see it this way, blame began to loosen from him, from my husband, from myself.

What looked like failure was simply the system responding.

Long before the mind understands what is happening, the body often registers the change. There were days I felt uneasy without being able to explain why. Though nothing obvious was wrong, something felt off. I could sense it before I could locate its source. Emotion followed later.

The body itself is a system. It is made of parts that constantly respond to one another. Cells react to chemical signals. Organs adjust to pressure. Rhythm begins to change before pain appears. When balance changes, the body notices before language can explain it.

I see this in my patients. A body is never only joints and muscles. It is sensation, memory, and belief moving together. I can work with someone whose strength has returned and whose balance tests well, and still watch them hesitate.

Often the instability is not mechanical. It lives in belief. Fear of falling changes how a person moves. Steps shorten. Posture stiffens. Reach narrows. That fear alters the nervous system, which alters balance, which then confirms the fear. What began as a thought becomes structure.

When belief becomes certain, the body follows. When the body settles, strength shows itself differently. I have watched people walk more steadily not because their muscles changed, but because their confidence did. The equation was never only physical.

Underneath whatever name we give these experiences, the same thing is happening.

That is why peace often leaves before collapse becomes visible. Tension can build before anything on the surface appears broken, as if structure were changing faster than thought could keep up.

Nature makes this easier to see. Roots redirect toward water when conditions change. Soil chemistry adjusts. A small shift at the root alters what the tree can support.

We are living systems nested inside larger systems, influencing one another at the same time.

When our son began to regulate, the change did not stop with him. Our home grew quieter. Mornings became calmer. Conversations slowed. Our other children settled more easily, and my husband and I stopped pulling in opposite directions.

A change in one place moves through everything connected to it.

When a new policy was implemented at work, the change did not stay on paper. It moved into our finances, our decisions, our sense of safety, and eventually our geography. What appeared as a single requirement reorganized an entire life.

When we reshaped how our children learned, structure changed first. Attention followed. Effort felt different. The household adjusted around that new rhythm without needing to be managed.

Loss revealed a truth I had not yet measured, and my future quietly reorganized itself around that recognition.

By then, these experiences no longer appeared separate. The body, the family, the work, the loss, the recovery. They were the same movement appearing at different scales.

This is why equations have never felt static to me. They do not sit on a page waiting to be solved. Once they are placed inside life, they move. They respond. They absorb pressure and redistribute it as conditions change.

I have watched equations contract under fear and expand under safety. When one variable settles, the whole structure breathes differently. When strain is relieved at the source, movement returns everywhere else.

To me, equations are alive because they behave like something alive. They adapt. They interact. They carry information forward. They exist inside other equations and are changed by them in return.

This is what appears in bodies, in families, in work, in loss, and in healing. The math never stood apart from life. It moved through it.

When truth is placed correctly inside a small equation, it does not stay there. It enters every larger equation it touches. The movement may be quiet. The effects may take time. But the direction is already set.

This is why I trust structure more than outcome. Why I watch conditions instead of chasing results. Why peace often arrives for me before anything on the surface has changed. I can see the equation holding, even when the result has not yet appeared.

To live this way is to know that you are never standing outside the equation watching it unfold. You are already inside it, influencing and being influenced at the same time.

If you are always living inside equations that continue moving beyond you, what does it mean to remain aligned when resolution may never arrive?

Recognizing that something is out of balance does not stop the equation from moving. The systems we live inside continue adjusting as conditions change, long before we recognize which variable has changed. Because every part of a system is connected, pressure moves through the structure and reveals imbalance. What matters then is not stopping the movement, but learning how to remain aligned with truth while the equation continues unfolding.

Chapter 20

The Return

I have learned that the need for space often comes from moments of overwhelm, when the movement inside our home becomes hard to manage. Too many things are happening at once. Nothing is technically wrong, but everything feels full. In those moments, the need for space is simply the need for the pressure to ease, even briefly.

There are times when awareness arrives without warning. It comes as weight. A sense that life continues moving whether I am ready or not, carrying me forward inside something larger than my awareness.

Being a mother to a child with autism means living inside questions that will not resolve in my lifetime. I do not get to imagine a future that eventually settles into certainty.

The awareness of that reality is always present. It grows heavier whenever I turn my attention toward it.

When I sit with uncertainty, it settles in my body as a dull ache. The weight of not knowing whether I will still be there when he needs me most.

That uncertainty does not stay contained in one child. It moves through all of my children. Through our home. Through the choices we make and the ones we delay. It becomes part of the equation I live inside every day.

What holds me is not the promise of answers.

It is knowing that order has not disappeared simply because the equation is incomplete. I live inside uncertainty, but not outside of truth. Something constant remains, holding what I cannot control even when I cannot see how it will resolve.

The fear does not disappear.

But I am no longer without footing beneath it.

There comes a moment when peace is no longer something I chase in my thoughts. It begins to appear in ordinary ways, something I recognize before I understand.

Sometimes, on long drives to see patients, I find myself in places where the world grows quiet. No traffic. No signs. Just open fields and trees standing where they have always stood, not rushing or competing, simply being what they are.

Each time I drive those roads, something in me settles.

My problems are still there, but the stillness in nature reminds me that truth still holds, even when my life feels unsettled.

That is when I realize it is not escape I am craving.

It is return.

Nature does not hurry or adjust itself to meet expectations. It moves according to what it is. In that order, I am reminded of what balance feels like when nothing is resisting what is already true.

People return and say they wish they could live there forever. What they are responding to is not the place itself, but the feeling it restores in them. The sense that things are as they should be.

In nature, nothing is trying to be something else.

The river follows its course.

The tree moves through its season.

The sun rises as it always has.

Nature lives within structure. Something in us recognizes that alignment as peace.

That is balance.

That is truth expressed inside an equation.

I have come to see that we do not go to these places to find ourselves. We go because they remind us of something we have lost. Our sense of alignment with the structure that holds everything together.

Returning to life after moments of stillness can feel difficult. Our responsibilities remain the same. What has changed is what we notice. And something in us feels the difference.

The feeling is not a sign of failure. It is feedback.

It tells us that something in our equation needs correction. Not through force or escape, but through alignment.

What we experience there is not escape.

It is recognition.

The recognition that I am not broken.

That my equation is out of balance.

And that correction is possible.

Problems may tip the scale out of balance.

Wherever truth is restored, even quietly, one variable at a time, the equation moves back toward alignment.

If math is the mechanism of peace in nature, I sometimes wonder why we resist applying it to our own lives. Why we treat our problems as the one place where structure no longer applies.

Nature does not get to choose what we do inside the equation.

We do.

That is the gift and the weight of being human.

Peace is not given to us or taken away. It appears when we stop forcing variables and allow truth to take its proper place.

The equation is already in motion.

The only variable left to choose is our own.

Free will.

Free Will × Alignment with Truth = Peace

Author Reflection

If you have made it this far, you may recognize parts of your own life in these pages. Most readers arrive carrying questions. Some come from pain. Others come from moments that never fully settled into understanding. Each of us enters with different variables already in motion.

This book did not begin as a study of mathematics. It began with noticing patterns.

Over many years I started seeing similar structures appear in very different places. I saw them in physical therapy, in the way the body responds to injury and recovery. I saw them in families, in the way relationships move through tension and repair. I saw them in the way emotion rises when something in a situation does not seem to make sense.

What kept appearing was not disorder.

It was structure.

For a long time people have said that life is not perfect. I understand why that idea can feel comforting. It creates distance from disappointment and pain. But it never settled in me as true.

What I began to see instead was that life unfolds the way equations do. Variables interact. Conditions meet other conditions. Outcomes grow from what is already in motion.

In that sense, life is structurally complete, even when what emerges from the equation is painful. The system responds exactly as the variables allow it to respond. What often appears chaotic may simply be an equation whose full set of variables we cannot yet see.

Human beings were given something remarkable: free will.

We can act, choose, and introduce new variables into the systems we live inside. But we were also given limits. Our senses are narrow, and our understanding is partial. We observe events and quickly assign meaning, even when we do not yet see all the conditions involved.

There is truth, which we may never fully see, and there are interpretations formed from the fragments available to us. Much of the tension we experience comes from confusing our interpretation of the equation with the equation itself.

The equations in this book are not meant to solve life. They are attempts to name patterns that already appear in ordinary experience.

Emotion is not dismissed in this framework. It often appears as the first signal that something in a situation feels strained or misaligned. But emotion does not organize the structure underneath an event. It responds to it.

When emotion becomes the conclusion instead of the signal, the equation closes too quickly.

Much of what this book attempts to do is slow that moment down. It creates space to look again, to notice variables that may not have been visible at first, and to allow the structure of the situation to reveal itself more clearly.

Healing does not always come from solving the equation. Sometimes it comes simply from knowing that there is one.

That recognition is often where healing begins.

Math heals in a subtle way. Not because it solves every situation, and not because it removes pain, but because it reminds us that life is not chaos. Even when we cannot yet see the full equation, it still exists. The variables continue interacting within a structure we may not yet recognize.

Recognizing this changes how we respond. The need to force immediate answers becomes less urgent. The pressure to resolve everything at once begins to ease.

We begin to see that the equation is still alive. It continues adjusting as conditions change and as new variables enter the system.

Nature moves within structure effortlessly. Rivers flow, trees grow, and ecosystems rebalance when conditions allow.

Human life carries something additional. We observe. We interpret. Sometimes we resist the structure in front of us. At other times we begin to recognize it.

That recognition changes how we move through the equation.

No single book can hold every variable. Life extends far beyond any framework that could be written on these pages.

Your equations will continue. New variables will appear. Others will resolve. Emotion will keep signaling. Truth will remain, even when it is difficult to see.

If something in these pages helped you notice the structure already present in your own life, that noticing can continue beyond this book.

Math Heals was never meant to be a finished system.

It is simply an invitation to remain curious about the equations unfolding around you and to allow time to reveal the variables that are not yet visible.

Your equations will not look like anyone else's. Each life carries its own history and conditions moving through time.

What comes next belongs to you.

An Invitation

Continuing the Conversation

Life often feels complicated in the moment it is happening. Emotions rise, explanations multiply, and a situation can begin to feel larger than we can hold.

In mathematics, complex problems are rarely solved all at once. They are simplified first. A larger equation is often reduced to smaller ones that can be understood clearly before the full solution appears.

Life can work in a similar way.

When a situation feels overwhelming, the first step is not always to find the answer. Sometimes it is simply to step back and ask a simpler question.

What is the most basic thing that can be seen clearly here?

From that starting point, the larger structure often begins to reveal itself.

The situations described in this book represent only a small portion of the kinds of equations people encounter in everyday life. Many readers will recognize patterns from their own experiences that were not described in these pages.

If you wish to share a situation from your own life, whether it is something you are still trying to understand, something that eventually resolved, or something you now see differently after reflecting on it, you are welcome to do so at:

MathHealsMindset.com

Situations readers choose to share may help inform future writing and projects that continue exploring how structure appears in ordinary human struggles.

Often the equations that trouble us most are simply the ones whose variables are not yet visible.

Discussion Questions
An Invitation to Observe

1. What situation in your life currently feels unstable or unresolved?

2. If you were to describe that situation as an equation, what are the known variables involved?

3. What outcome keeps repeating, regardless of how the situation is approached?

4. Which variable have you been treating as fixed that may actually be adjustable?

5. What information or constraint might still be missing from the equation?

6. What small change could you test to see how the structure responds?

7. What would you watch for to know whether alignment is increasing or decreasing?

Appendices

On Perspective
Appendix A

The chapters of this book describe experiences as they unfold in ordinary life. Situations appear, reactions follow, and understanding grows gradually through attention over time.

The appendices take a different step. Rather than continuing the narrative, they pause to look more closely at the structure that became visible within those experiences.

The language used throughout the book carries specific meaning within that structure. Words such as variable, alignment, correction, and probability are used deliberately, not as metaphors, but as ways of naming relationships that appeared repeatedly across different situations.

Perspective plays an important role in seeing those relationships clearly. A moment viewed from within emotion can appear chaotic or unfair. The same moment viewed across time may reveal patterns that were not visible while the experience was unfolding. Perspective does not change what happened, but it can change what becomes visible about it.

These appendices step slightly outside the narrative in order to clarify the language and structural observations that emerged from it. They do not introduce a method to follow or a system to apply. Instead, they explain how certain ideas function within the framework presented in these pages.

What follows describes the language, relationships, and symbolic structure that appear throughout the book.

Beyond the Numbers
Appendix B

Many people think mathematics is simply the study of numbers. In school we often encounter math through calculation, so it is easy to assume that numbers are its primary focus.

In reality, mathematics is broader than that. At its heart, it studies patterns, relationships, and structure. It explores how parts of a system interact, how variables influence outcomes, and how certain conditions lead to particular results.

Some areas of mathematics do focus on numbers, such as number theory. Other branches examine structure in different ways. Algebra studies relationships between variables. Geometry examines shapes and spatial relationships. Analysis explores change and continuity. Set theory considers how mathematical objects relate to one another.

Mathematics begins with simple starting points called axioms. From these assumptions, mathematicians use careful reasoning to see what must follow. Over time, consistent patterns emerge within the system.

Because mathematics studies structure and relationships, it has long influenced how people think about the world.

The scientist Galileo Galilei once wrote that the universe is written in the language of mathematics, suggesting that nature itself follows patterns that can be described mathematically. Later, René Descartes argued that clear reasoning could reveal order beneath confusion. Still later, Bertrand Russell explored how mathematical logic might help clarify complicated ideas.

Their work was not an attempt to reduce life to numbers. Instead, it reflected the belief that reality often contains underlying structure that careful thinking can bring into view.

This book approaches life from a similar perspective.

The equations that appear throughout these pages are not meant to be literal formulas for living. They are ways of noticing relationships, observing how choices, conditions, and experiences interact to shape outcomes.

When life feels confusing, it is often because one or more variables are hidden or not yet understood. Looking at a situation from a different perspective can reveal that what once felt chaotic may contain its own form of order.

In that sense, mathematics becomes a way of noticing patterns in human experience. And sometimes, noticing the structure is enough to begin understanding.

Language of the Framework

Appendix C

This book uses familiar words in specific ways to observe how they function when life is viewed through structure rather than reaction.

What follows briefly clarifies how certain terms are used within these pages.

These meanings are not universal claims. They are the internal language of this work.

Some of the language below appears throughout the book in equation statements. These equations are collected later exactly as they appear, without explanation or expansion.

They are not formulas to apply. They are structural observations already present in life.

Foundational Conditions

Order

Order refers to the underlying structure by which reality operates.

Order is not imposed. It is observed. It exists before explanation and remains after interpretation.

Constant

A constant is that which does not change.

In this book, truth functions as a constant. Order does not adjust itself to preference, emotion, or belief. It exists whether we acknowledge it or not.

Structural Elements

Equation

In this book, an equation names structure rather than a problem to be solved.

An equation represents how elements relate, how causes produce effects, and how outcomes emerge from what is already in motion.

The equation exists whether it is noticed or not. Writing it down does not create it.

Variable

A variable is any element that can change without altering truth itself.

People, circumstances, choices, environments, timing, and capacity can all function as variables.

Variables are neutral. Misalignment occurs when a variable is treated as a constant, or when too much weight is placed on a single variable to carry an entire outcome.

System Behavior

Alignment

Alignment is the state in which variables cooperate with truth.

Alignment does not guarantee ease, success, or immediate resolution. It produces coherence. Over time, alignment allows outcomes to organize themselves without force.

Misalignment

Misalignment occurs when variables are arranged in opposition to truth, or when essential variables are missing from awareness.

Misalignment provides information. It signals that structure is being ignored, misread, or overridden.

Correction

Correction is the natural movement that follows misalignment.

Correction reflects cause and effect restoring balance. It does not require intention or belief.

Probability

Probability, in this book, refers to truth carried forward through time.

The future does not emerge from hope, fear, or imagination.

It emerges from what is already in motion.

When structure is present, outcomes begin organizing themselves long before they can be seen.

Human Participation

Free Will

Free will refers to the capacity to respond within structure. It does not grant control over outcomes.

Free will allows testing, adjustment, and responsibility. It does not override truth.

Emotion

Emotion functions as a signal. It indicates alignment or misalignment but is not part of the equation itself.

Emotion responds to structure. It does not define it.

The Mathematics of Emotional Signals
Appendix D

Emotion functions as feedback within a system, much like a measurement taken by an instrument.

When the instrument is properly calibrated, the signal is informative. When calibration is disrupted, the signal may become distorted.

Not every emotional signal reflects the equation precisely. Noise can enter the system and affect how feedback is registered.

This does not invalidate emotion as information, but it does require care in interpretation.

As equations grow more complex, especially those involving larger systems, emotional signals may appear before the structure becomes clear. Multiple variables may be active at once, increasing the likelihood of misreading.

Human perception also shapes interpretation. Emotions are named through individual lenses formed by experience, expectation, and context. The same imbalance may be perceived differently by different observers.

For this reason, emotional specificity should guide inquiry rather than conclude it. Signals narrow the direction of investigation. Observation and testing bring clarity.

As variables are identified more accurately, interpretation improves and alignment becomes easier to recognize.

Emotion provides information. Precision reveals structure.

The Mathematics of Emotional Signals

Signal	Indicates	Look For
Anger	Force applied against perceived violation or constraint	Boundary errors, withheld truth, restricted agency
Fear	Unstable or missing constant	Unknown variables, unreliable structure
Anxiety	Excess active variables without order	Competing inputs, lack of hierarchy
Sadness	Loss of expected variable or outcome	Removed inputs, changed conditions
Grief	Permanent loss of foundational variable	Equations requiring restructuring
Guilt	Perceived imbalance of responsibility	Misassigned ownership, unequal ratios

Signal	Indicates	Look For
Shame	Identity misidentified as variable	False self-conclusions, structural misattribution
Frustration	Effort no longer affecting outcome	Saturation, limiting constraints
Confusion	Undefined or unclear relationships	Missing definitions, hidden assumptions
Resentment	Prolonged imbalance without correction	Delayed truth, avoided adjustment
Relief	Resolution of uncertainty	Restored constants, clarified structure
Peace	Sustained truth–structure alignment	Stability, equilibrium

These signals do not define the equation. They narrow the direction of inquiry. Structure becomes clear through observation, testing, and correction over time.

Balance and Misalignment in the Equation
Appendix E

In the chapter on emotion, feeling was described as the mark beside the work. The ✔ or ✗ does not change the equation. It only indicates whether the steps align with truth.

Looking more closely, another question appears: why does emotion arise in an ordered system at all?

When alignment exists, peace appears.

Peace = Truth × Alignment

When misalignment exists, peace cannot be the result.

Peace ≠ Truth × Misalignment

Emotion points to that difference. It signals that something in the structure of the equation requires attention.

There is another layer worth noticing.

Emotion is not only a signal that something has changed. It is the natural indicator that appears when the balance of the equation moves out of alignment.

A simple way to picture this is a scale.

When weight is added to one side, the scale tips. The tilt does not mean the scale has failed. It reveals the difference between the two sides.

Human emotion often functions in a similar way.

When the variables in a situation move away from alignment, tension appears. That tension is what we experience as distress.

Distress = Truth x Misalignment

From the perspective of order, the equation itself still holds. The system continues responding to the variables present.

What we experience emotionally is the feeling of that loss of balance.

Emotion does not belong inside the equation. It is not one of the variables being solved. It functions more like the indicator on a scale, moving when balance changes and drawing attention to where alignment has been lost.

If the indicator were missing, the imbalance would still exist, but it would be harder to notice.

Emotion serves that role in human life. It makes movement within the equation visible.

When alignment exists, emotion often confirms it through a sense of peace.

When misalignment exists, emotion signals that the current variables cannot produce that peace.

The structure itself remains consistent. Reality continues responding to the variables present.

When the variables align with truth again, the equation resolves.

Reading the Equations
Appendix F

The equations in this book describe structure that became visible through attention over time.

They describe structure that became visible through attention over time.

An equation, as it appears here, names a relationship that already exists. It names a relationship that already exists. The purpose is not to change life by using the equation, but to recognize what life is already doing.

These equations describe relationships rather than numerical calculations. Their form expresses structure rather than arithmetic equivalence.

Numbers in mathematics are absolute. Words are not.

The terms used here carry defined meaning within the framework of this book, but they do not behave like numerical symbols. Rearranging them may illuminate meaning, but reduction is not their purpose. Each term holds its place within a defined structure. Removing or substituting terms outside that structure alters the relationship being described.

In traditional algebra, equations represent numerical equality between interchangeable quantities. Because those quantities share the same mathematical form, the equation can be rearranged or transposed.

For example, if

$$A = B + C$$

one may isolate a term and write

$$B = A - C$$

or

$$C = A - B.$$

These operations remain meaningful because the symbols represent quantities of the same type.

The equations in this book function differently. They describe relationships within a system rather than interchangeable numerical values. The elements on each side represent different kinds of conditions operating within the same structure. Because these elements are not interchangeable units, algebraic operations such as subtraction or transposition do not produce meaningful interpretations.

In this framework, the equal sign represents alignment rather than numerical identity. It indicates that the elements on both sides correspond within the structure being described. When that alignment holds, the system remains stable. When it breaks, imbalance appears.

In nature and in the body, relationships function in the same way. Systems operate through interaction between distinct elements that cannot simply be rearranged. The relationship between oxygen, circulation, and the heart, for example, cannot be meaningfully transposed as though those parts were variables on a chalkboard. Each element holds a specific role within the system.

Some readers may wonder why equations are used at all if they are not meant to be manipulated algebraically. Mathematics provides a clear language for expressing relationships and balance. Symbols such as the equal sign and the plus sign do not belong exclusively to arithmetic. They are used across many sciences to describe how elements within a system relate to one another.

In many fields, equation-like expressions are used conceptually rather than computationally. Biology, psychology, and systems science often describe relationships using symbolic structures that resemble equations but are not meant to be rearranged or solved. These expressions make patterns visible and show how balance emerges from interaction.

The equations in this book serve the same purpose. They are visual descriptions of structure. The format allows relationships to be seen quickly and clearly, highlighting how elements align within a system and how imbalance appears when that alignment changes.

The equations presented here are intentionally general. They describe patterns that appear across many situations rather than the full specificity of any single life.

In lived experience, equations are often more detailed. Variables are named more precisely. Conditions become clearer. As an equation becomes more specific, it becomes more faithful to reality.

When variables are identified accurately, it becomes easier to distinguish structure from reaction, and truth from emotion or perception.

Emotion appears when an equation is under strain or when alignment begins to break. It signals change, but it does not explain it.

Precision brings clarity.

Equations do not exist in isolation. Each one sits within others across different scales.

A pattern observed in a body may also appear in a family. A change within a household may reorganize work, place, or future. Scale alters form without changing structure.

For this reason, the equations in this book serve as entry points. They help reveal where additional variables are present, where conditions apply pressure, and where alignment or misalignment is unfolding over time.

To read these equations well is not to solve them, but to notice them.

To see when repetition becomes information.

To recognize when effort no longer changes outcome.

To observe how systems respond as variables change.

Alignment grows from naming equations more accurately and remaining attentive to structure as it reveals itself over time.

Structural Equations
Appendix G

The following equations appear throughout the chapters of this book. They are gathered here as they arise within the narrative.

They are not formulas to apply or steps to follow. They describe structural relationships observed in the situations discussed in these pages.

The specific variables present in any life will differ. An equation that appears in one situation may not appear in another.

What remains consistent is the presence of structure itself.

Order − Witness = Truth

Being Human = Truth + Free Will

Truth + Observer = Experience

Emotion ≠ Truth

Emotion = Feedback

Clarity = Truth × Time × Endurance

Comfort − Clarity = Instability

Outcome = x + y + z

Known Variables − Missing Variable = Instability

Unknown Variable + Test = Information

Equation × Choice ≐ Growth

Effort + Desire = Outcome

Repetition = Pattern

Pattern + Action = Alignment

Alignment + Structure = Healing

Attention + Truth = Awareness

Truth × Time = Probability

Truth × Structure × Conditions = System Alignment

Love = Order × Grace

Love = Truth × Proportion

Forgiveness = Alignment Verified Over Time

Peace = Truth × Alignment ✓

Peace ≠ Truth × Misalignment ✗

Free Will × Alignment with Truth = Peace

These statements are not meant to resolve anything. They are meant to be seen.

Mathematical Operators in This Framework
Appendix H

This glossary explains how mathematical operators are used symbolically within the *Math Heals* framework.

The operators retain their mathematical meaning while being used to describe structural relationships within human experience. They do not create meaning. They clarify relationships that are already present.

+ Addition

Meaning: Combines variables within the same structure.

Example: Effort + Desire = Outcome

Use: Indicates contribution. Multiple variables participate in producing an outcome.

− **Subtraction**

Meaning: Removes or isolates a variable from the equation.

Example: Comfort − Clarity = Instability

Use: Indicates interference, absence, or reduction of influence. Subtraction often reveals how removing clarity or structure produces instability.

× **Multiplication**

Meaning: Links variables in a reinforcing relationship.

Example: Truth × Time = Probability

Use: Indicates interdependence. Each variable strengthens the overall result. Multiplication shows that the relationship between variables matters as much as the variables themselves.

÷ **Division**

Meaning: Filters or reduces a variable through another factor.

Example: (Not used directly in the book's equations.)

Use: Division can describe situations where perception, misunderstanding, or constraint limits what becomes visible within a system.

= Equals

Meaning: Indicates structural identity between cause and outcome.

Example: Alignment + Structure = Healing

Use: Shows the result produced when variables interact within a stable relationship. The equals sign does not imply control over the result. It reveals the outcome produced by the variables present.

These symbols do not create meaning. They provide a consistent language for observing how structure operates across situations.

Acknowledgments

To my family, who heard these thoughts long before they were written, thank you for listening, even when I would not stop talking.

To my friends, who have been my sounding board, who came and went, and to those who remain through every season.

To everyone I met and every experience along the way, thank you for what each encounter taught me.

And above all, to God, the Author of all order and truth. Everything true in this book already belonged to Him.

About the Author

Tiffany Suson is a home health physical therapist and homeschool mother of five, including a child with autism. She has practiced physical therapy for more than two decades in a variety of rehabilitation settings, including thirteen years working inside patients' homes.

Her approach to rehabilitation is holistic, integrating traditional physical therapy with yoga and tai chi alongside an ongoing interest in spiritual growth and reflection.

These experiences ultimately inspired the ideas explored in *Math Heals*.

AFTER ALL THINGS

To God, the Author of all truth,
the One who revealed what is real
and gave freedom its promise.

*"You shall know the truth,
and the truth shall set you free."*

— John 8:32

www.ingramcontent.com/pod-product-compliance
Lightning Source LLC
Chambersburg PA
CBHW031024160726
47991CB00005B/1862